# The
# DEVA
# HANDBOOK

## How to Work
## with Nature's
## Subtle Energies

### NATHANIEL ALTMAN

Destiny Books
Rochester, Vermont

Destiny Books
One Park Street
Rochester, Vermont 05767

LIBRARY OF CONGRESS CATALOGING-IN-PUBLICATION DATA

Altman, Nathaniel, 1948–
The deva handbook: how to work with nature's subtle energies/
Nathaniel Altman.
p. cm.
Includes bibliographical references.
ISBN 978-0-89281-552-4
ISBN 0-89281-552-3
1. Angels.  2. Nature—Religious aspects.  3. Human ecology—Religious aspects.
4. Mental healing.  5. Theosophy.  I. Title.
BP573.A5A57  1995
291.2' 15–dc20      95–10774
CIP


Printed and bound in the United States

10  9  8  7  6  5  4

This book was typeset in Optima with Cuento as the display typeface

Destiny Books is a division of Inner Traditions International

# The DEVA HANDBOOK

# Contents

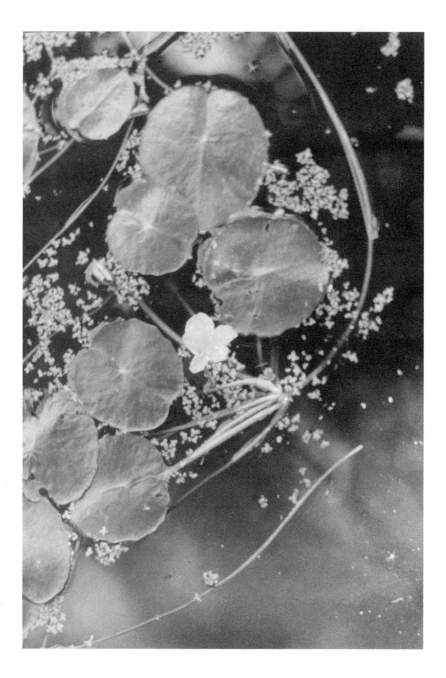

# Preface

I first became interested in devas while working as a groundskeeper at the national headquarters of The Theosophical Society of America in Wheaton, Illinois, after graduating from college in 1971. During that summer I met Geoffrey Hodson, who describes his clairvoyant investigations into the devic realms in *The Kingdom of the Gods* and other works. He later became my mentor during his tenure as instructor at the Krotona Institute School of Theosophy in Ojai, California, the following year.

My interest in devas increased through my work as coauthor of *Finding Your Personal Power Spots* with Jose Alberto Rosa, M.D. (The Aquarian Press, 1985). Jose had become involved with devas in the Brazilian countryside, where, as a therapist, he often conducted workshops and retreats. He discovered that by helping others find the "power spots" within their bodies and in nature, they would be able to achieve a deeper level of personal groundedness and self-understanding. While he received direct insight into the subject through firsthand experience, my primary role as coauthor was to conduct additional library research and present the material in an organized way. Though I often felt inspired by Jose's work, I didn't believe that I would ever be able to communicate with devas myself.

My first conscious experience with devas, however, took place several years later when I was writing *The Nonviolent Revolution* (Element Books, 1988). I was experiencing difficulty writing a chapter about nonviolence toward the environment. As I gathered material about the harm humans have done to the land, air, waters, plants, and animals, I got more and more discouraged. I was beginning to feel that there was no hope to save the planet from environmental destruction, which resulted in a powerful case of writer's block. Although the chapter was to be in the middle of the book, it was the only chapter I had not written; I had focused instead on other chapters I felt more comfortable with.

With the publisher's deadline fast approaching, I decided to go to a favorite spot in a forest by a waterfall in upstate New York. Although at the time I didn't believe that I could communicate with devas (I believed that only clairvoyants like Hodson could do that), I hoped to be inspired by the beauty of the waterfall and the surrounding area. Pen and paper in hand, I spent the entire afternoon writing down ideas for the chapter, which seemed to flow to me endlessly. I also realized that these ideas did not originate from my conscious mind. I later put many of them into the chapter, which I felt was both down-to-earth yet inspiring.

Yet it was not until the summer of 1990 that I began to communicate with devas in earnest. I was experiencing a period of emotional distress, which manifested as depression, fatigue, and various physical aches and pains. Being a confirmed hypochondriac at the time, I believed that my physical discomfort was a sign that I didn't have very long to live. Needing a break from the stresses of New York City, I decided to spend a week alone in French-speaking Canada.

One morning I decided to visit the Montréal Botanical Garden. I arrived there feeling sad and somewhat vulnerable, and began walking through the gardens, stopping from time to time to examine the trees and other plants more carefully. At one point I found myself sitting by a small lake under the shade of a grove of willows. One of the trees had a sturdy main trunk that grew horizontally to the ground before arching upward toward the sky. Judging by the smooth bark on the upper side of the trunk, it was a popular climbing tree, since the trunk was easy to climb and could support the weight of several adults. I was instinctively drawn to the tree, and I suddenly climbed onto the trunk and lay my entire body astride it. I then hugged the tree with all my strength, wrapping both my arms and legs around the trunk. With deep emotion and a total lack of self-consciousness, I fervently asked the tree for help, not consciously knowing what type of help I wanted.

Suddenly I experienced a strong shift in consciousness in which I felt that the whole world was alive. I also felt an increased awareness of nature. Instead of seeing myself as an observer, I felt myself as an integral part of the natural world. I especially felt a deep energetic connection to the tree, along with a powerful lifting of my spirits. After a few minutes I climbed down from the tree and lay beneath it on the grass. Later I thanked the tree and then went walking slowly through the gardens, which seemed more beautiful than ever.

During my stroll, I experienced the sensation that the flowers were greeting me. After returning home later in the week, I continued to feel drawn to flowers. I took a pen and notepad to a neighbor's garden. Though it was still difficult to believe that a flower would want to communicate with me, I decided to suspend judgment and be open.

After admiring a bright purple petunia and spending a few minutes in quiet contemplation, I began writing whatever came into my consciousness. I was left with the following passage:

> What you see when you look at me is a being of tremendous complexity and depth. I have the Divine Essence pulsating through me; the violet richness of Divine Light! It comes from the very core of my being and is moving outward through my petals. Your veins are also pulsing with the Divine. It comes from the core of your being. From your very roots, from what you call the seat of the Kundalini Fire. This energy is your life.
>
> Yet all too frequently it is not fully realized. It is neither truly acknowledged nor understood. In addition, this Divine energy is often blocked, so it flows incompletely through your being. It may move to certain parts of you, but it is partial. Yet it is still beautiful, even in its incompleteness. Incompleteness represents a hope, a striving, a potential. It should not necessarily be labeled as "bad."
>
> Consider this point carefully, for all life is movement. You are not less perfect for being less complete, as it were. The major goal for you—both individually and collectively—is *the movement*. To appreciate and cherish your incompleteness as you strive for completeness. Incompleteness is your highest stage of being at this very moment. Yet you need to embrace the movement of life as you strive toward a greater, more evolved state of completeness.

I was soon spending a good part of the summer months visiting flowers in parks, gardens, and vacant lots throughout Brooklyn. I received simple and uplifting messages about the role of flowers in the world, spirituality, and ecological consciousness. I believed that if I could access inspiration, wisdom, and guidance from plants in an urban area like Brooklyn, people could do so anywhere in the world. I collected the messages in a notebook I called "Brooklyn Spirit Garden," and fragments of a number of these messages are included in this book.

Later that year I continued this work in the old-growth forests of Chile, Argentina, Costa Rica, and the United States. By consulting with the devas about how human beings could work to save the planetary environment, I felt I would be learning from the very source. For several months I visited trees, rivers, cliffs, lakes, and even a volcano, and asked the resident devas, "How can humans work to save the environment?" The messages I received fill several notebooks. While visiting a grove of yellow beech trees in Chile, I was inspired to write *Sacred Trees* (Sierra Club Books, 1994). I later extended my visits to devas in the western and eastern United States. *The Deva Handbook* was inspired during a visit to a five-hundred-year-old white oak tree near New Hope, Pennsylvania, during the summer of 1991.

The basic format of *The Deva Handbook* was guided by devas, and a portion of the material presented comes from them. This doesn't mean that the book is a faithful reflection of devic wisdom. As a human being with my own ideas, conditioning, and experience, I cannot say that my own impressions do not come into the picture.

I do know, however, that at this particular point in planetary (and human) history, all beings of the world must unite to prevent the Earth from experiencing further environmental destruction. As the most powerful animal species on the planet, we hold the keys to both planetary destruction and planetary healing. This gives us a unique opportunity to help actively to heal the Earth. Working with the powers of nature—as personified by members of the devic kingdom—is a fundamental aspect of this effort.

Though imperfect and incomplete, I feel that much of the material presented here can be useful in helping us to connect with, learn from, be healed by, and cocreate with nature's subtle beings.

Brooklyn, New York
July 1995

# PART ONE

# GROUNDING

# 1

# Who Are the Devas?

*Power, life, light; these are gifts which companionship with the angels*
*shall place in human hands. Power that is limitless; life that is*
*inexhaustible; light before which all darkness melts away.*
**—Geoffrey Hodson, Devas and Men**

When we take a walk in nature, we observe many things. Our walk can take us over hills and valleys, or through meadows covered with thousands of wildflowers. We may jump from rock to rock as we cross a rushing stream, or cool our feet in the waters of a mountain lake. Our journey may take us through deep forests, homes to trees that have been standing for hundreds of years.

When surrounded by nature, our perceptions often go beyond the awareness of our five senses. When we experience the beauty of a waterfall, the majesty of a tree, or the fragrance of a wildflower, most of us, at one time or another, have perceived "something else": feelings of peace, comfort, healing, or protection. We often have come back from a walk in nature with new inspiration, unexpected solutions to difficult problems, and fresh insights into our life and relationships.

Native traditions throughout the world have taught that in addition to responding to the outer beauty of a waterfall, a tree, or a flower, we often perceive the inner realms of existence that are connected to these outer forms. These energies are believed to take subtle physical bodies that are rarely seen but are often sensed through intuition. They are known by different names: angels, nature spirits, fairies, sylphs, *orishas*—or by the Sanskrit term *devas,* meaning "the shining ones."

Devas can be defined as forms, images, or expressions through which the essences and energy forces of the Creator or Great Spirit can be transmitted, or forms through which a specific form of Earth energy or life force can be transmitted for a specific purpose. Although both humans and devas channel and direct energy, devas are believed to follow an evolutionary path that is distinct yet parallel to our own. Like us, they choose the Earth as a home where they can live and work, and as the place to gain wisdom and life experience.

## THE ANGELIC HIERARCHY

The human perspective on devas traces its roots to our earliest recorded history. Devas have been variously portrayed in the Bible, the Koran, the Vedas, and the Bhagavad Gita—and in myths and legends from ancient Greece and Rome, from countries including Mexico, China, and Japan, and from throughout Africa and Oceania—as messengers, members of a heavenly court, helpers, groups of warriors, sources of healing power, guardian angels, and spirit guides. They have been considered luminous energy principles that stand behind all phenomena, and they work both with nature and with the cosmos to guide the evolution of life.

There are literally thousands of different types of devas, ranging from the tiniest wildflower dryad to the greatest solar archangel, and the realm of the devas is as vast as the universe itself. In India, devas are seen as primary reflections of the One Infinite Godhead, the source of all creation in the universe. Religious and metaphysical literature has described the most important devas as solar archangels of incredible size and power, who oversee the evolution of the solar system and the planets. In Western literature, sun gods include Aloah va Daath (Cabalistic), Apollo and Helios (Greek), Ra, Horus and Osiris (Egyptian), Balder (Norse), and Lugh, Dagda, and Hu (Celtic). In the East, the early Japanese worshiped the solar archangel as the goddess Amaterasu-oko-mi-kami, the Maoris called him Tamanuitera, and the Vedas referred to him as Surya, "the one eye of what exists that looks beyond the sky, the earth, the waters."

The solar archangels are assisted by planetary archangels, who are associated with each planet in the solar system. Planetary archangels are a synthesis of all the archangels, angels, and nature spirits who exist within the planetary field. Here on Earth, the planetary archangel has been known by many names: Often referred to generically as the "Earth Mother," she was known as Gaia by the Greeks, Chomolungma by the

4

Tibetans, Pachamama by the Incas, Rinda by the Norse, and Tailtiu by the Celts.

Planetary archangels are assisted, in turn, by angels connected with the evolution of the four elements: fire, earth, air, and water. These great "angels of the elements" are aided by devas who guide the evolution of different plant, animal, and insect species, as well as every group, division, and classification of rock and mineral. Such devas would be connected to what is known to occultists as a "group" soul, standing behind the instinct and intelligence of different animal species. A group soul involved with bees, for example, would stimulate the natural instinct of bees to fly, look for food, pollinate flowers, build and maintain their hives, protect themselves from predators, reproduce, and observe a blueprint of social organization that is uniquely their own.

Other types of devas are connected to different religions and are entrusted with the duty to assist in the spiritual unfoldment of the sect's devotees. The literatures of many of the world's religions (including the Cabala, the Bible, the Vedas, the Popul Vuh, and the Koran) have spoken extensively of this type of archangel. Perhaps the most striking contemporary reference was recorded by Joseph Smith, the nineteenth-century American who founded the Church of Jesus Christ of the Latter-Day Saints, who was visited by the angel Moroni. In *The Book of Mormon*, Smith writes:

> He called me by name, and said unto me that he was a messenger sent from the presence of God to me, and that his name was Moroni; that God had a work for me to do. . . . He said there was a book deposited, written upon gold plates, giving an account of the former inhabitants of this continent, and the source from whence they sprang. He also said that the fullness of the everlasting Gospel was contained in it, as delivered by the Savior to the ancient inhabitants.

Many major religious and historical events (such as the appearance of the archangel Gabriel on the *mir' aj* or Night of Ascension, of the prophet Mohammed and the intervention of the archangel Michael, staying the hand of Abraham who was about to kill his son, Isaac, as a sacrifice) have taken place through the intercession of devas. Lesser angels who are associated with these great archangels are connected to individual places of worship and are attracted to any place where a religious service is held, whether it is a church, synagogue, mosque, or longhouse, a shelter for the homeless, a home altar, or an outdoor celebration of the beginning of spring. These devas are said to channel love, wisdom, healing, and inspiration to all those who take part in the service.

In addition to angels of religions, many believe there are also angels who reign over each nation of the world. They channel their unique energy to strengthen the particular "keynote quality" of each individual nation, and assist in the evolution of those who choose the particular nation as their arena of life experience. There are also angels of love, will, harmony, wisdom, movement, form, building, destruction, music, beauty, and healing. The archangel Raphael, for example, is the best-known healing deva in Christianity, while Omolu is considered the orisha of healing among those who practice the Candomblé religion in Brazil. In Hindu mythology, the *mahadeva* ("great god") Shiva, is an angel of the first order. In his role as destroyer, Shiva destroys in order to allow matter to regenerate on a higher plane of existence.

In addition, certain archangels are believed to govern the progress of great epochs of human evolution and cultural development, and channel their unique energy for the benefit of humanity. In *The Mission of the Archangel Michael*, the mystic and philosopher Rudolf Steiner describes how the period of the Renaissance (1510–1879) was inspired by the archangel Gabriel, whose keynote energy was that of incarnation. During the period of his strongest influence, humanity was involved in exploratory voyages, scientific, cultural, and economic development, and the populating of the Earth. The present epoch (since 1879) is guided by the archangel Michael. Steiner believed that part of Michael's mission involves leading humanity from a materialistic, earthbound way of living toward a more spiritual existence, yet without abandoning our primal connection with the Earth.

Some Western religions teach of the existence of guardian angels: a personal deva who guides us and protects us throughout our life. In Exodus 23:20–21, Yahweh declares to Moses: "Behold, I send an Angel before thee, to keep thee in the way, and to bring thee into the place which I have prepared. Beware of him and obey his voice . . ." Guardian angels have long been recognized as guides who help oversee the processes of our personal evolution, and offer us guidance, support, and comfort as we tread the often difficult path of living in the day-to-day world.

# DEVAS OF NATURE

In addition to the devas who form the upper echelons of the hierarchy of angelic beings, there is also a great variety of devas connected to nature. Because these are the devas who most often associate with human beings, they will be the primary focus of our discussion in this book.

Opinions vary regarding what constitutes a deva as opposed to a nature spirit; these sometimes represent two different expressions and functions within nature. Machaelle Small Wright, the founder of the Perelandra Garden in rural Virginia, says that a deva represents a more "universal and dynamic" aspect of consciousness, which, like an architect, organizes and creates natural forms. A "nature spirit," by contrast, is "an intelligent level of consciousness within nature that works in partnership with the devic level and is responsible for the fusing and maintaining of energy to appropriate form. Nature spirits are regional and attached to specific land areas."

Other researchers disagree, contending that devas are indeed connected to specific land areas. In *The Kingdom of the Gods* and *Clairvoyant Investigations,* Geoffrey Hodson refers to devas as being attached to specific trees, mountains, rock formations, and parks. (One of his most interesting stories describes how the Cornwall Park Deva in Auckland, New Zealand, sends devic energy to a nearby hospital, assisting both patients and physicians. In *Clairvoyant Investigations,* Hodson observes that "physicians who are sufficiently responsive [to the deva] sometimes receive guidance in the form of tendencies to respond to instinctual ideas—especially when a mystery exists concerning the patient's condition.")

Although the distinction may be valuable from an intellectual perspective, we will not be concerned about the differences between devas and nature spirits in this book. In many cases, the terms will be used interchangeably. Since both devas and nature spirits share devic consciousness, our goal is to commune with and work with any members of the devic realms who wish to accept our love, respect, and cooperation. As we will see later on, subtle nature beings have different functions and powers, and many assist each other in myriad ways. A large deva connected to a major mountain range will most likely have a wide variety of devic assistants working harmoniously with it. Some can be classified as "elementals," which assist the larger devas at a very basic level, not unlike the way worker bees assist their queen.

*Villarrica Volcano, Chile*

If we are privileged to work with a subtle nature being, it means that we are resonating with its energy. Therefore, we will attract the appropriate nature being according to our sincerity, our energy level, and the work that we are intended to do together. From my point of view, it does not matter whether we commune directly with a powerful deva connected to a large mountain, a nature spirit overseeing a grove of trees in the foothills, or a tiny elemental involved with the evolution of a flower growing beside a mountain path. Though different, all of these subtle nature beings are part of *one consciousness*. By having the desire to commune with them from a place of love and respect, we will naturally attract the most appropriate nature being at the proper time.

## FOUR BASIC TYPES

Generally speaking, subtle nature beings fall into four main groups related to the four primary elements of creation.

# Earth

Nature spirits of the Earth are connected to all land-surface areas, including fields, mountains, deserts, rock formations, and land surfaces that lie beneath the water. They are linked to the formation and evolution of the chemical components of minerals, the building stones of the Earth's crust. Because humans are land-based beings, earth devas are most likely to interact with us, and are therefore considered the best-known members of the devic realm. Like other nature spirits, devas associated with the Earth can vary in size and power; devas connected to fields and outcroppings of rock can range between several inches to several feet in size, while an earth deva who stands behind the evolution of a high mountain can be twice as large as the mountain itself.

"Dryads" make up one variety of nature spirit, and are connected primarily to trees and other members of the plant kingdom. Like other devas of nature, their power and size depend on the physical form with which they are associated. Certain highly developed dryads may be involved with the evolution of an entire forest, rather than with individual trees alone.

# Water

Nature spirits connected to water are known as "undines." They are found in (and above) oceans, lakes, rivers, streams, and waterfalls. Their size and power varies according to their level of evolution, location, and life task. For example, the deva associated with a place like Niagara Falls has been described as a magnificent luminous being several hundred feet tall, whose breadth spans the cataracts on both the Canadian and American sides. In folklore, undines have often been depicted as female, although clear male and female differences do not generally apply to devas.

# Fire

Nature spirits of fire are known in Greek and Sanskrit mythology as "salamanders." They are connected to the energy of the Sun, and would be found primarily in places in nature that receive the fullest sunlight, such as beaches and deserts. Because devas are the "energetic framework" around which physical matter takes its form, salamanders would actually manifest along with fires within the Earth (such as volcanoes and other places of thermal activity), as well as with lightning and fires in general. In Mayan mythology, for example, the god Kakupacat—who was believed to manifest through volcanoes—would be considered a salamander along with the god Kinichkakmo, who was associated primarily with surface fires and fire in general.

## Air

In Cabalistic literature, air elementals are known as "sylphs," and are said to be connected with the formation of clouds and the laws that govern the movement of wind. If you were to go to a very windy place (be it the top of a building or a cliff overlooking the sea) chances are that you would be in the realm of the sylphs.

Sylphs have been depicted in folklore and metaphysical literature as being colorful, somewhat human in size, and moving through the air at great speeds. In China, they were personified by Feng Po, the god of winds, who was depicted as an old man with a white beard, wearing a yellow cloak and blue and red cap; in his hands he holds a sack containing wind. In *The Kingdom of the Gods*, Geoffrey Hodson describes sylphs as winged beings. He adds, "As they wheel and fly across the wide arch of the heavens, brightly colored forces flash with extreme rapidity between and all about them, but more especially in the air above."

It is important to remember that the devas representing these four elements in nature rarely exist separately. If you were to visit a waterfall, for example, you would be visiting the realm of nature spirits connected to flowing water (the falls itself), the Earth (the rocks over which the water flows), and, most likely, the wind. In addition, devas often interpenetrate each other energetically, since they work together to fulfill their tasks in nature.

Because nature spirits are connected, in various ways, to every aspect of earthly creation (including the winds, rain, mountains, rivers, trees, shrubs, flowers, grasses, algae, cliffs, and rock formations), there are far more of them than we can consciously imagine. While there has never been a "deva census," some students of devas speculate that they can easily number in the billions, and that there are probably more devas populating the Earth than humans and other animals combined.

# WHAT DO THEY LOOK LIKE?

The appearance of nature spirits is very subjective, and a similar type of deva may be portrayed differently by people of different cultures. For example, dryads in Irish folklore have usually taken on the appearance of leprechauns, while dryads on the South Island of New Zealand have been described as resembling early Maori warriors. Devas will also appear different according to the individual who observes them, because each of us has a unique perspective on life based on genetics and acquired knowledge or cultural conditioning. We know that if two artists were to observe the same tree, in all likelihood their portraits of the tree would be very different. Even two scientists, when considering the same chemical or biological phenomenon, often have different interpretations of the same event. The same appears to be true when two people consider the appearance of a deva. In addition, the deva's form can vary considerably, and can change at will.

In Japanese folklore, a deva connected to a sacred plum tree was depicted as a beautiful maiden, while in Homer's *Odyssey* the nymph Calypso appears as "a shining goddess" dressed in a "gleaming white robe, fine-woven and delightful." In the Afro-Brazilian religion Candomblé, Oshounmare, the androgenous deity of rainbows, is depicted as both a valiant warrior and beautiful woman, wearing yellow beads with green stripes, a multicolored turban, and a ritual garment made of green embroidered muslin. A contemporary description of a deva observed clairvoyantly was offered by Geoffrey Hodson in his book *Man's Supersensory and Spiritual Powers*:

> There are various layers of force within the auras [energy fields] of the angels, each layer with its own hues and direction of flow. The general effect is of brilliantly-colored, shot moire silk, composed of flowing forces, rather than of solid substance, and in constant, wave-like motion. Through these many . . . emanations, from within outward, streams of radiant energy, often white and of dazzling brightness, are continually flashing.

Because most humans have not yet developed clairvoyant sight, the primary way we can sense the presence of a nature spirit is through intuition. In this way, we are able to focus more on the "essence" rather than the "form" of the deva. While being able to see the splendor of their subtle forms can be among the greatest experiences a human can enjoy, the fact that we do not see devas does not mean that we cannot acknowledge their presence and work with them for our mutual benefit. By the same token, we cannot see electricity, but we are aware of the tremendous importance it plays in our daily life.

## WHERE ARE THEY FOUND?

Because they are connected to the natural processes of nature, earth devas are traditionally depicted in remote areas that are not normally inhabited by human beings, such as forests, mountaintops, desert areas, and isolated regions near the North and South Poles. However, they can be found anywhere on the planet where life springs from the Earth, especially in important geographical features like waterfalls, mountains, volcanoes, cliffs, rivers, and lakes, even if these places are surrounded by human inhabitants. They are also found in parks, tree groves, and gardens of all kinds, even in large cities. Devas are especially present wherever there is intense weather activity, such as windy places, and are connected to the formation of rainbows, storms, and tornadoes.

Many of the most dramatic physical features of the Earth have long been considered to be the homes of the world's most majestic nature spirits, and have been important "power spots" for both local people and international visitors alike. Many are the subjects of myth and legend. The Aborigines, for example, have always believed that Uluru (Ayers Rock) is a sacred earth temple and a center of earthly magnetism and fertility, while Mount Everest is traditionally considered to be the home of the Earth Mother by the Tibetans. Ancient Hawaiians believed that the Mauna Loa volcano was the home of the goddess Pele, while Hindu mythology teaches that the goddess Ganga transformed herself into the Ganges River, which flows from the big toe of the god Vishnu, "The Preserver." There are probably hundreds of such power spots on Earth. Some of the largest (and best-known) of these places include the following mountains, volcanoes, canyons, lakes, rivers, and waterfalls in different continents of the world:

## North America

Mount McKinley-Denali (Alaska)
Grand Canyon (Arizona)
Death Valley (California)

Mount Shasta (California)
Pike's Peak (Colorado)
Mauna Loa Volcano (Hawaii)
Copper Canyon (Mexico)
Niagara Falls (Ontario and New York)
Crater Lake (Oregon)
Mount Hood (Oregon)
Mount Ranier (Washington)
Old Faithful Geyser (Yellowstone National Park, Wyoming)
Mount Logan (Yukon Territory)

## Europe

Stonehenge (England)
White Cliffs of Dover (England)
Mont Blanc (France and Italy)
Eldfell and Helgafell Volcanoes (Iceland)
Mount Vesuvius (Italy)
Naerodal Pass (Norway)
Mount Elbrus (Russia)
Mer de Glace (Switzerland)

## Asia

Huanggoushu Falls (China)
Ganges River (India)
Mawsmai Falls (India)
Mount Hebron (Israel)
Mount Fuji (Japan)
Khone Falls (Laos and Kampuchea)
Annapurna (Nepal)
Mount Everest (Nepal and Tibet)
Lake Baikal (Russia)
Valley of Geysers (Russia)

## South and Central America

Lake Nahuel Huapí (Argentina)
Mount Aconcagua (Argentina)
Iguassu Falls (Brazil and Argentina)
Torres del Paine (Chile)
Irazú Volcano (Costa Rica)

Galápagos Islands (Ecuador)
Mount Chimborazo (Ecuador)
Machu Picchu (Peru)
Lake Titicaca (Peru and Bolivia)
Angel Falls (Venezuela)

## Africa

Nile River (Egypt)
Lake Victoria (Kenya, Tanzania, and Uganda)
Table Mountains (South Africa)
Tugela Falls (South Africa)
Mount Kilimanjaro (Tanzania)
Victoria Falls (Zambia and Zimbabwe)

## Oceania

Ayers Rock-Uluru (Australia)
Mount Kosciusko (Australia)
Mount Jaya (Indonesia)
Mount Cook-Aorangi (New Zealand)
Rotorua Geysers (New Zealand)
Wangerei Headlands (New Zealand)

Nature spirits can also be found in abundance in the major wooded areas of the world, including the redwood forests and sequoia groves in California, the rainforests of Brazil, Central America, and Indonesia, and the vast coniferous forests of Alaska, Canada, Scandinavia, and Russia.

# WHAT DO THEY DO?

Nature spirits reveal the hidden, formative life that works within (and through) all living things in nature. They are, in essence, an agent through which Divine Energy manifests and are a "blueprint" that enables this energy to express itself in the physical world. In addition, devas serve as a type of transformer that "steps down" this cosmic energy and wisdom to a frequency that is usable on a physical level.

As channels of Earth wisdom and Earth energy, they stand behind the evolution of mountains, rock formations, lakes, rivers, oceans, trees, and other plants. Through the wisdom we refer to as "the laws of nature," they govern creation, adaptation, and growth as they relate to the four elements of fire, air, earth, and water. They play a role in the self-cleansing of a lake, the photosynthesis of a tree, the growth of mosses and seaweed, and the intense thermal activities of an erupting volcano. Devas are involved with the laws that govern the movement of winds, and they play a role in the formation of rain and other weather patterns. In essence, nature spirits assist in the fundamental processes of life's creation and help preserve and protect the integrity and harmony within the area of Earth we know as the biosphere.

Devas have been regarded as nature's specialists, and they may perform either a single function or a variety of different tasks. Some aid in the processes of building and creating new forms (including setting the limits to the form's growth and development), while others deal with the destruction of old ones.

Machaelle Small Wright created the famous Perelandra Garden in Warrenton, Virginia, through the guidance and cooperation of many devas, including a being she identifies as Pan. In the *Perelandra Garden Workbook*, Wright recounts Pan's message that "In each garden, there is a crew of nature spirits assisting the process of soil building and improving. The emphasis of their work is the fusion of the soil building pattern into the soil and assisting the unfolding and movement of that pattern."

Some devas offer inspiration, while others provide protection. Some facilitate communication and the sharing of information, while others are involved with tasks of repair and healing. Although largely overlooked and unrecognized, devas are very much a part of the world we live in.

## DEVA-HUMAN COMMUNICATION

Most of us are instinctively aware that devas exist, although few of us have ever actually seen one. In our early years of childhood, we subconsciously sought out their presence in "special" areas of our world: Many of us had a favorite tree in the backyard or a particular outcropping of rocks in the park we visited when we wanted to daydream or read a book. Those of us who lived in the country may have had a special grove of trees we ran to in the woods when we were upset and wanted to be alone. While we were at summer camp, some of us would spend hours at a spot by the shore of a lake where we would dream about the future. While we were in these special areas, we may have experienced sensations of comfort, calm, and a sense of feeling accepted. Some of us even

*The Favorite Tree, Los Angeles, California*

had "invisible friends" in the forest or garden, with whom we conversed and played. If you experienced such perceptions and feelings, chances are that you were in contact with one or more of the devas who were connected to these places.

Devas can communicate with human beings in a variety of ways. Some people with clairvoyant sight are able to perceive the devas' subtle physical forms. Others "hear" devas, and record their messages through their own voice or by writing. Some people feel inspired to draw pictures that represent the essence of information received from nature spirits. However, the vast majority of us can perceive communication through intuition. By cultivating our innate human powers of observation, curiosity, and respect, we can learn how to become more open to the world around us, including the subtle realms of the devas. It is also important to remember that devas often offer us "seed thoughts" and other types of subtle contact. Although we may not feel the impact of this interaction at the time we are in nature, we may be able to perceive it later on, especially while we are in a dream state.

Human-deva cooperation can manifest itself in a number of important areas. Because they are intimately connected to the evolution of natural life, devas can teach us how to understand nature and help us appreciate our place in the natural world. They help us appreciate the tremendous variety of natural forms and show us how to respect both the wisdom that created these forms and the life force that animates them. Devas can offer practical advice regarding conservation, environmental protection, reforestation and forest management, farming, landscaping, design and maintenance of parks and other green spaces, and the proper use of plants for healing and inspiration.

Devas can also help us to experience a greater sense of harmony with our natural selves and to find the security, sensitivity, and wisdom this implies. They help us to discover what makes us uniquely human, yet they allow us to stay in contact with our natural "animal" essence and instincts. For many of us, this is completely uncharted ground, although it is a goal that we deeply seek. Working with devas can help us to walk on the Earth in balance with sensitivity and respect.

Devas, furthermore, can channel the innate healing qualities of nature. By learning how to commune with them, we can access their powers of protection, comfort, and healing. They help us to strengthen the qualities of courage, truth, and compassion in ourselves and assist us in manifesting these qualities in our daily lives. Finally, devas can help us to better align our body, mind, and emotions so that we become more in harmony with both our inner and outer worlds.

When we seek to commune and cooperate with the subtle beings in nature, *they* benefit as well. We assist them in fulfilling their tasks of creation, evolution, and integration, especially as these apply to defending, protecting, and helping to heal the Earth. We provide devas with insights and perspectives that are uniquely human, and we offer them a realm of experience they need for their own evolution.

Because we are a living part of this planet, contact with the subtle forces of nature is our birthright. By reestablishing our lost connection with subtle nature beings, we aid in the process of healing both ourselves and the Earth on whom we live.

## THE CHALLENGE AND THE OPPORTUNITY

Of all the issues that confront humanity, there is no greater concern than the survival of our planet. As a great living body providing food, shelter, and sustenance, the Earth is essentially—as the Native Americans have taught—our "mother" in the deepest and fullest sense of the word.

In spite of her vastness, strength, and generosity, Mother Earth is being abused by humans unceasingly. Vast forests are being destroyed at a rate of thousands of acres a day; pollution from cities, factories, and automobiles chokes the rivers, lakes, and air; land erosion renders once-fertile soil barren and contributes to poverty and starvation in many parts of the world. Many believe that if these trends are not reversed, the Earth will cease to be able to support the human population, let alone the other animals and plants who share this home with us.

At this critical moment in planetary history, a growing number of human beings are beginning to devote their energies toward saving our planetary home. Efforts in environmental education, recycling, conservation, and reforestation are moving at a rapid pace. An increasing number of people are seeking to "return to their roots" and reclaim our lost connection to the land and the natural wisdom it provides. They are also trying to reconnect with their "animal" nature through shamanistic and neoshamanistic traditions—such as ceremonial drumming, chanting, vision quests, and ingesting psychotropic plants—with the hope of bringing themselves closer to natural wisdom, deep intuition, and the ability to respond to Earth energy and Earth rhythms.

According to Dora Van Gelder Kunz, whose clairvoyant powers were described in Shafica Karagulla's book *Breakthrough to Creativity,* the primary task of the devas is to transmit and direct force. Although their focus is on the Earth as a whole rather than specifically on humanity, they direct this force toward those of us whose energy is in synchronicity with theirs and who are ready to receive it. She says that as the number of individuals involved with environmental protection increases, so will the opportunities for deva-human communication.

Since devas are clear and powerful channels of Earth wisdom, they can provide us with the perspectives, approaches, and information necessary to live harmoniously with nature, and to develop viable long-term strategies to aid in the Earth's preservation and healing. They are an unrecognized and underutilized resource in our efforts to save the planet. In fact, they can be our most powerful ally in educating us to know what the Earth needs and how those needs can best be met.

## 2

# Devas and Humans: Our Forgotten Connection

*What nature says to us awakens something deep within our hearts.*
*The angels speak in joy, of joy and eternal things, even in the midst*
*of their concern for how humanity is affecting their work on Earth.*
*They remind us of our destiny as builders, not destroyers, of the*
*whole of the planet. They urge us to a greater unfolding. Their*
*message is one to listen to, embrace, and act on.*

**—Dorothy Maclean, To Honor the Earth**

The relationship between humans and devas can be traced back to the dawn of human history, and this connection has been an integral part of native religious teachings in many parts of the world. Nature spirits were acknowledged and revered in ancient Egypt, Greece, Japan, China, India, and Rome, and are still a part of many cultural traditions like those of the Australian aboriginals, the Shuar of Ecuador, the Cuna of Panama and Colombia, the Maori of New Zealand, as well as the Navaho, Ojibway, Cholula, and other native people in North America. Priests in ancient Greece used to sleep under the oaks of Dodona to receive wisdom from nature spirits they called dryads, while practitioners of Candomblé in Africa would visit a river to ask the deva (known as Oshoun) for her blessing and protection before taking marriage vows. The mythology of Native Americans, as well as that of the Celts, Egyptians, Greeks, Jews, Chinese, and Japanese, is filled with stories of "talking" trees, healing waterfalls, sacred stone chambers and circles, magical groves, and holy mountains. In Greece, the sky god, Zeus, was said to communicate with mortals through the sacred oaks of Dodona, where priests and priestesses would go to consult the oracle by interpreting the rustling of the leaves. A similar belief was shared by the Tlahuica of Mexico, who believed that local trees whispered to them when the wind rustled their leaves. In fact, the Tlahuica symbol for speech was a tree with three branches, which was later adopted as the official seal of the city of Cuernavaca.

Throughout human history, devas connected to these natural forms have been recognized as potent sources of Earth wisdom for those who are open to their messages. Rather than being considered superstition, communion with the subtle forces of nature is viewed as a practical way to access Earth wisdom and healing power, and enable humanity to live in harmony with the rest of the natural world.

This Earth-centered approach contrasts with dominant cultural beliefs regarding our relationship with nature, which teach that there is a clear separation between heaven and earth as well as between body and spirit. Christianity in particular opposes pagan (or "natural") religious belief, which teaches the transformative and inspirational qualities of nature. In preliterate times—and in many native cultures today—inspiration and magic have been considered normal aspects of everyday life. Whether people are hunting, healing, harvesting food, or journeying into expanded realms of consciousness, traditionally they have viewed nature as both teacher and healer in which magic is an essential aspect of existence.

Although there have been Christian mystics such as St. Francis, Julian of Norwich, and Teresa of Avila, who were intimately connected to nature, Christian patriarchs emphasized the sharp division between the natural and the supernatural. Over the centuries, this split eventually became so large as to nearly deprive nature of the inner spirit that Earth-centered religions like Druidism, Shinto, Taoism, and Aboriginal and Native American beliefs have taught breathes through all things.

Concurrent with the influence of Christianity on the Western view of nature, the intimate relationship our ancestors enjoyed with the natural world became lost as humanity became more "civilized." As we migrated to the cities and suburbs, we began to lose touch with nature. After the beginning of the Industrial Revolution in particular, we felt so divorced from the natural world that we began to believe nature was our servant, to manipulate and exploit as we wished. The final outcome has been a callous insensitivity and disregard toward the environment. The whole-sale destruction of forests, the slaughter of the buffalo, the defiling of the land by strip mining, the chaotic growth of suburban housing, highway construction, and industrial development, and the pollution of the air, rivers, oceans, and lakes are reflections of the fact that we do not feel part of the living environment or respect the other living beings who inhabit the natural world.

## THE EARTH: A LIVING BEING

Robert (Medicine Grizzlybear) Lake, a traditional Ojibway healer and ceremonial leader, believes that the continued economic exploitation of the Earth is causing a serious planetary imbalance that can no longer be ignored. He believes that unusual weather patterns, volcanic eruptions, increased earthquake activity, record-breaking snowstorms, floods, droughts, pestilence, and new diseases are all reactions to the violation of the Earth by humanity. He writes, "Mother Earth is not only becoming polluted, but is also becoming weak and very sick. . . . If she dies, we all die. It is as simple as that." The increasing rates of cancer, birth defects, and diseases related to lowered immune levels among humans and other animals testify to the compromised health of the Earth as a whole.

Ancient tradition teaches that the Earth is a living body, and that all that exists on Earth shares in a powerful, all-encompassing life force that vitalizes and mobilizes every aspect of our planetary home. The ancient Polynesians called this force *mana*, the early Hindus spoke of it as *prana*, the Algonquins knew it as *manitu*, and the Omahas called it *wakanda*. The followers of Shinto, the traditional religion of Japan, called it *kamikaze*, or "divine wind," based on *kami*, meaning the elemental powers permeating all natural phenomena, and *kazi*, the wind, which is what animates the kami's powers. During the Second World War this term was adopted by Japanese aviators who flew suicide missions against the Allied naval forces.

The Blackfeet, who are native to the state of Montana, believed that this power was a gift from Natos, the Sun, and was the creative source of all power and animation. They call this power "Great Spirit" and believe that it is found in mountains, winds, animals, and trees. The Sun has long been venerated by the Blackfeet, and in turn, Natos blesses them for respecting all of his creations.

Elders in indigenous cultures throughout the world have taught that there is no such thing as an "inanimate object" in nature, and that the gift of life is shared not only by two-legged, four-legged, and winged creatures, but by plants and soil, rivers and lakes, cliffs and mountains, rain

*Ayarrán grove, near Angosturas, Argentina*

and winds. These are not seen as separate from humans, but rather they are viewed as our "relatives" (often our older relatives). Human life must therefore be considered within the total context of all of the children of the Earth Mother.

The religious traditions of our earliest ancestors were based on the belief that the Earth is both a living being and a "mother" to all life forms that exist on the planet. The belief in a nurturing mother was the foundation for goddess worship, which existed long before the worship of male gods. Traces of goddess worship have been found in archaeological records and artifacts in Siberia, southern Africa, and Ireland, some dating as far back as 25,000 B.C. The prehistoric great Goddess was the forerunner of the goddesses we read about in ancient myths and legends.

Examples of the all-powerful goddess include Ajysyt, the Siberian goddess of birth, Nammu from Sumeria, and Omeciuatl in Mesoamerica. To the ancient Greeks, the Earth was the goddess Gaia, and the continents of Africa, Asia, and Europe were named after Gaia's other manifestations. Nokomis was the Earth Mother of the Algonquin people of North America, who believed that all living things were nourished from her bosom. The Kaean people of New Guinea know her as Dzari, while descendants of the Aztec know her as Toci, the Mother of the Gods and the Heart of the Earth. Among the Maori of what is now New Zealand, Papatuanuka (Papa) was the name of the Earth Mother, and her son, the god Tanemahuta (Tane), created the "Multitude of Trees" in order to cover her nakedness.

Among the early Slavic peoples, Gaia was called Mati-Syra-Zemlya and was regarded as a supreme being. According to anthropologist Stanley Krippner, peasants would dig a small hole into the soil with their fingers, put their ear over the hole, and would listen to what "Moist Mother Earth" had to tell them.

Because the Sun and the Earth Mother were so great and all-encompassing, our ancestors came to isolate and personify different aspects of "Great Spirit." Like the Blackfeet, they often worshiped the Great Spirit through the smaller, more tangible forms they could see and feel like mountains, lakes, rivers, stones, animals, insects, and plants.

Like humans, trees exist primarily in the vertical dimension. This is one reason they have long held a special place in our relationship with natural forms. As living creatures that are a mighty manifestation of life, trees provide nourishment, protection, medicine, fuel, and shade. They have also offered beauty, hope, comfort, and inspiration to humanity from our very beginnings. Many early cultures believed in a cosmic or mythical tree that stood at the center of the universe, while others

*Pine trees, Victoria Island, Argentina*

believed that humans were actually born from trees. Nordic mythology, for example, teaches that the first human male was born of the ash tree, while the first female was born of the elm.

Because our early ancestors—and many native peoples today—lived in close proximity with nature, they were often directly exposed to the challenges of natural phenomena like storms, earthquakes, and volcanic eruptions. For that reason, nature was both revered and feared, and the early human beliefs about nature gods and other spirits were strongly influenced by these experiences. For example, animal and human sacrifice can be viewed as a way to placate angry gods and nature spirits in places like Mexico and Polynesia, where devastating volcanoes and earthquakes occurred on a regular basis.

The fear of nature was not universal, however. Many native cultures saw nature not as something to be feared, but rather as a special friend and benefactor. In her essay "Notes on the Indians' Belief in the Friendliness of Nature," anthropologist Frances Densmore wrote in 1948 about an Ojibway elder named Ruffled Feathers who often worked with water spirits. When asked whether the presence of waves on a river indicated anger on the part of the spirit, he replied:

> Waves do not mean that the Water Spirit is angry with those who wish to cross. It is natural that there should be waves in rough weather as well as smooth water, but if the Water Spirit is asked by the right person, he can quiet the waves at that time so the people can proceed in safety.

According to The Encyclopedia of Religion, "There is hardly any object in the natural cosmos that has not become the center of cult somewhere at one time or in one place or another." In addition to worshiping divinities of the heavenly realms, the followers of Shinto worshiped gods of the air (including wind gods, storm gods, and rain gods) as well as gods of the Earth. Sea gods, plant gods, river gods, and mountain gods, including Oho-yama-tsu-mi, the "great lord of the mountain" who was served by countless lesser nature beings, were especially revered. In a geologically unstable region like Japan, the early human inhabitants also worshiped (and feared) nature gods of the underground, who were considered responsible for earthquakes and volcanic eruptions.

Respect and reverence for fire gods was strong among the Maori, and ritual fires have long played an important spiritual function in many

Maori tribes. The Tuhoe, for example, celebrate more than twenty-eight different ceremonies that involve ritual fires. They include Ahi Taitai, a fire over which a prayer is chanted to protect the life principle in humans, and Ahi Torongo, a ritual fire designed to invoke the gods' protection over the sweet potato crop from destruction by caterpillars and grubs.

The Hindus have long worshiped nature beings, and ancient Vedic hymns often personified the forces of nature and endowed them with human characteristics. For example, Indra is a Hindu storm god who figures prominently in the Rig-Veda. As a god whose storms can bring both fertility and destruction, he has always been both loved and feared. The Vedas also speak of rivers as "mothers" and "protectors," while prayers in the Vedas are offered to the mountains, the winds, and the Earth. The massive mountains of northern and central India have long been personified by Hindus, and were admitted to the rank and station of great gods in Vedic times.

The Hindus have also traditionally worshiped fire spirits, river spirits, and tree spirits. Both the pipal tree and the banyan tree are considered the abode of gods Brahma, Vishnu, and Shiva—the Creator, the Preserver and the Destroyer, respectively. Many other trees (including the mango, bel, neem, jujube, and kadamba) are all considered to be the home of various gods and goddesses.

The Celts of pre-Christian Britain and Gaul had a powerful tradition of nature worship that was especially focused upon sources of water, including rivers, lakes, and springs. The Celtic terms *deva*, *diva*, or *devona*, meaning "the divine," were often ascribed to rivers. Borvo, Burmo, or Mormanus were the names given to the "boiling" god of thermal springs. Because sacred waters gave growth to trees, the Celts believed that trees were sacred as well, and were often the homes of tree gods. The god Fagus was connected to beech trees, Boxenus to box trees, and Robur was the deva of oak trees.

The Druids—a priestly sect among the Celts—maintained sacred groves as their primary temples of worship. In fact, the Gallic-Brittonic term *nemeton*, or sanctuary, implies a sacred oak grove or clearing in the woods. Along with the yew and the birch, the oak (held sacred to Thor), was part of the Trinity of Trees corresponding to the Druid's Three Pillars of Wisdom. Special enclosures of stone, wood, or timber were often built around sacred springs (like that surrounding the thermal springs of Les-Fontaines-Salées in Yonne, France) and sacred hills (such as the Hill of Tara in County Meath, Ireland). Although much speculation centers on the true function of the famous temple at Stonehenge, some researchers—

including the eighteenth-century architect John Wood—believe that it was primarily a temple for Druidic sun worship.

Like the Celts, the Teutons, who lived in what is now Germany, viewed tree groves as sanctuaries that were homes of friendly spirits. As in other parts of the world, sacred groves were often connected to sacred springs, for water was universally considered as a source of spiritual power. In addition to springs, the Teutons worshiped rivers, streams, wells, and waterfalls from a perspective of gratitude and friendship. The winds of the forests were often feared, however, because the Teutons believed that the winds were the spirits of the dead riding out on the Wild Hunt.

The early Estonians felt a special kinship to the forest, which they viewed as a living being infused with supernatural power. Many early Estonians were farmers, hunters, and gatherers, and lived outside of the forest's realm; however, they viewed the forest as a place to escape from enemies as well as to obtain food in the forms of animals and plants and to collect valuable wood for construction, cooking, and heating.

Forest spirits are described in a story recounted in *Old Estonian Folk Religion* by Ivar Paulson:

> Every forest has its own spirits. The spirits of the birch forests never go to an alder or oak forest, nor do they go from one forest to another even if these are the same type. The spirits themselves are supposed to be of the good kind. They are said to harm no one. It is told that in olden times they were put into the forest to guard it. They sometimes threaten bad people and make them lose their way, such as the ones who chop wood on Sunday, who play crude jokes or who are up to no good.

Like many other early peoples, the Estonians developed a number of practices to maintain friendly relations with the overall spirit of the forest, as well as with the myriad lesser spirits (*metsavaimud*) found there. Offerings, given in exchange for benefits obtained from the forest, included "pledges of friendship": bands made of straw, leather, branches, or flowers that were tied around individual trees. This custom was especially used whenever an animal was killed for food, as an expression of gratitude and to help atone for the harm done to the animal.

In Central and South America, many native peoples worshiped nature. The Aztecs, for example, worshiped Tlaloc, the "Pulp of the Earth" and the god of mountains, rains, and springs. Each year, they would set up an artificial forest, with a large tree in the center surrounded by four other trees symbolizing the four directions of the world. The central tree was called Tota, "Our Father," and it represented Tlaloc in all his glory. It would eventually be taken from the circle and "planted" upright in the center of a lake, where a human (usually a young girl) was sacrificed in Tlaloc's honor.

The Polynesian people have long believed in nature spirits. Hawaiian shamans, or *kahuna*, teach that everything is alive, aware, and responsive, and that their god-self (the *aumakua*) is the source of this awareness. In *Kahuna Healing*, Serge King explains:

> A tree has its own *aumakua*, as does the forest of which the tree is a part, the valley in which the forest lies, and so on to the very world itself—and beyond. In the old days a kahuna would ask permission from the tree spirit before he cut it, or from the spirit of the valley before he crossed it. He did this out of respect for the same source that lived in all of them and in order to ensure cooperation.

The Australian aboriginals, considered to be the oldest surviving human culture, have traditionally believed that all living forms—including mountains, rivers, lakes, trees, animals, and humans—are imprints of the metaphysical or ancestral consciousness that created them, meaning that the physical cannot be separated from the spiritual. Like other indigenous cultures, the Aborigines believe that the Earth and the biosphere are populated by a vast number of spirit beings, including a powerful sky god known by the names of Baiaime, Daramulun, or Nurundere ("The Father of All Things"), rain gods like Wuluwaid and Bunbulama, and Koi, the spirit of the bush. According to Robert Lawlor in *Voices of the First Day*, "Animals and plants are considered the embodiment of the world-creating forces, the Dreamtime Ancestors. Their physical presence on earth represents the spiritual presence of the gods." For this reason, every aspect of tribal life traditionally has been connected to awareness of and respect toward nature spirits, an approach to daily living that continues to this day.

The Mapuche of the Patagonian regions of Chile and Argentina hold that the spirit of the sacred *pehuen*, or araucaria pine, not only provides food during periods of scarcity, but has a positive metaphysical influence on the harvest. It is considered to be especially kind to women and children. This tree is also said to be connected to a nature being known as "Hachas de Pillan," who dwells in the volcanoes of southern Chile. Like Zeus of the ancient Greeks, Hachas de Pillan is regarded by the Mapuche as the creator of storms and thunder.

Anthropologist Ziley Mora Penroz quotes an old Mapuche woman from the Quepe region of Chile who respects the spiritual aspects of nature in her daily life as a ceramist:

> When I go and collect black clay for making *metawe* [earthenware vessels], I always leave the *regkuse* [the feminine spirit of the clay] other small earthenware vessels or anthropomorphic figures made of the same clay. From time to time I leave some colored wool or good herbs. One can also sing and dance in her honor. If one doesn't do this, it is certain that something will happen to the *metawe:* either it will break, no one will buy it, or the black glaze won't work out.

A number of early Yoruba traditions of communing with nature spirits were brought to the Americas—from what is today Nigeria, the Congo, and Angola—by slaves during the sixteenth century. One of these is the religion of Candomblé, now practiced primarily by inhabitants of the northern coastal cities of Brazil, including Recife, Fortaleza, and Belem. A related tradition is the Afro-Caribbean religion of Santería, practiced widely among Cubans and Puerto Ricans of African descent (including Cubans and Puerto Ricans living in the United States). By leading devotees to come into deep contact with the forces of nature, these religions teach that we open ourselves consciously to the wisdom and healing power connected to rocks, mountains, streams, and lakes. They teach that working with the spirits that stand behind these natural forms empowers us and enables us to serve as a "bridge" between the forces of heaven and earth, blending spiritual vision with practicality and realism.

Both Candomblé and Santería teach that there is an all-powerful, all-encompassing creator god (known as Olorun) who is assisted by a vast pantheon of literally hundreds of different gods and goddesses. They not only assist in the evolution of nature, but also provide personal assistance to human beings. Each nature spirit, or orisha, is connected to a particular nature form.

## Major Orishas and Their Corresponding Forms in Nature

| Candomblé | Santería | Nature Form |
|---|---|---|
| Oshala (Oxalá) | Obatalá | Mountains |
| Yemanjá (Iemanja) | Yemayá | Ocean |
| Nanan (Naná) | Naná Burukú | Still freshwaters |
| Shangó (Xangó) | Changó | Cliffs |

| Oshoun (Oxum) | Ochún | Rivers, streams |
| Omolu (Omulú) | Elegguá | Fields; open spaces |
| Oshossi (Oxossi) | Ochosi | Forests |
| Ogun (Ogoun) | Oggun | Iron deposits |
| Yansan (Iansa) | Yansá | Winds |

Both Candomblé and Santería have developed elaborate and powerful ceremonies relating to each orisha. Special hymns, dances, costumes, personal preparations, prayers, religious figurines, and animal sacrifices (although some churches permit the use of plant-food offerings instead) all have a role in these ceremonies, which should be performed under the guidance of a qualified Candomblé or Santería priest or priestess.

## COMMUNION WITH DEVAS AMONG WESTERNERS

During the past several hundred years, sensitive individuals living in the industrialized Western nations—including prominent philosophers, musicians, religious leaders, poets, and artists—may have communicated with nature spirits from time to time. Although few of them have actually testified to having experienced contact with devas, the luminous paintings of landscapes and plants by artists like Vincent Van Gogh, Albert Bierstadt, Odilon Redon, Frederick Church, Thomas Cole and other members of the Hudson River School of painting reveal an almost supernatural connection with nature that goes beyond the traditional five senses. The writings of Henry David Thoreau, Ralph Waldo Emerson, Walt Whitman, John Muir, J. Krishnamurti, Jacques Yves Cousteau, Father Thomas Berry, and others also betray a connection with nature of unusual depth and sensitivity. In the final stanza of his poem "Fog," Thoreau writes:

> Spirit of lakes and rivers—seas and rills
> Come to revisit now thy native scenes
> Night thoughts of earth—dream drapery
> Dew cloth—and fairy napkin
> Thou wind-blown meadow of the air.

During the twentieth century, a number of people documented their association with nature spirits. Several of these people have been affiliated with the The Theosophical Society, an international organization

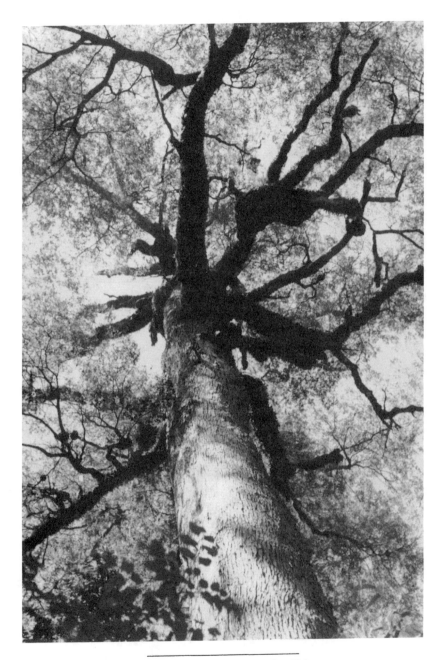

*Yellow beech tree, near Peulla, Chile*

promoting the study of comparative religion and investigating powers latent in nature. One of the earliest theosophical researchers was C. W. Leadbeater (1847–1934), a teacher and clairvoyant best known for his book about human energy centers, *The Chakras*. In *The Hidden Side of Things,* published in 1913, Leadbeater speaks about small nature spirits (popularly known as fairies) who often gravitate toward freshwater areas:

> Some very beautiful species inhabit inland waters where man has not yet rendered the conditions impossible for them. Naturally enough, the filth and the chemicals with which water is polluted near any large town are disgusting to them; but they have apparently no objection to the water-wheel in a quiet country nook, for they may sometimes be seen disporting themselves in a mill-race. They seem to delight in falling water.

One of Leadbeater's favorite students was Dora Van Gelder Kunz. Past president of The Theosophical Society in America and the developer of the popular healing modality known as Therapeutic Touch, Ms. Kunz is a noted clairvoyant who has been communicating with devas for more than eighty years. In he booklet *Devic Consciousness* she writes:

> The ways we look at life give us what is called "eye knowledge," seeing things out there, separate from ourselves. This leads us to make judgements based on our reaction to the external aspects of things. We see nothing but the form, which at once either attracts or repels us. Devas, in contrast, perceive life in terms of energies; to them the harmonics and rhythms of nature are most important.

Perhaps the best-known theosophical researcher has been Geoffrey Hodson (1886–1983), a teacher, writer, and healer who, like Leadbeater and Kunz, was highly respected for his clairvoyant ability. Hodson began communicating with members of the devic hierarchy in 1926, while hiking in the English countryside. During his lifetime, Hodson wrote more than sixty books, including ten on the angelic hierarchy alone. In the introduction to his celebrated book *The Kingdom of the Gods,* Hodson describes his clairvoyant observations of nature spirits:

> One day, as on a hillside at the edge of a beech forest in a secluded valley in the west of England, I was seeking ardently to enter the Sanctuary of Nature's hidden life, for me the heavens suddenly became filled

with light. My consciousness was caught up into a realm radiant with that light which never was on land or sea. Gradually I realised the presence of a great Angelic being, who was doubtless responsible for my elevated state. From his mind to mine there began to flow a stream of ideas concerning the life, the force and the consciousness of the universe and their self-expression as angels and as men.

He later describes a clairvoyant encounter with a very large deva on Bream Head Mount near the entrance to Whangarei Harbour in New Zealand. He describes the deva as somewhat human-shaped, more than four hundred feet high, and surrounded by an aura of energy measuring some one hundred yards. "The color is purple shot through with white fire, changing to green halfway up, and to yellow where the throat and heart would be." As if communicating to him, the deva explained some of its responsibilities:

Unlike my brothers, I am equally concerned with the evolving life-spirit in the air above and all around me, though more especially across the harbour entrance to the land beyond. Also, I am assisting in the evolution of the life in the mineral and plant kingdoms within this mount and over a wide range below.

The English physician Edward Bach (1886–1936), who developed the famous Bach Flower Remedies, was a highly sensitive individual who spent much of his time in nature. Bach believed that the Sun would transfer the essential electric "vibration" of flowers into water, which would become energetically impregnated as a result. By floating flower petals in spring water, he allowed the Sun's rays to infuse each flower. Through this ancient method, he developed thirty-eight different flower remedies that directly correlate to specific moods or mental attitudes—such as fear, anger, worry, anxiety, and envy—and serve as catalysts for the subtler levels of the healing process to take place.

While Bach himself made no claims to having communicated with devas in his research, contemporary practitioners like Molly Sheehan of Green Hope Farm in New Hampshire believe that devas not only guide her in selecting and preparing flower essences, but actually transfer the healing energy and wisdom from the flower petals to the water. When we ingest the remedies containing the flower essence, the vibrational quality of the flower—as governed by the flower deva—affects our subtle emotional and mental natures and allows us to achieve alignment and healing.

Perhaps the most important contemporary figure bringing the reality of devic and human communion to the general public is Dorothy Maclean, author of *To Honor the Earth* and a noted workshop leader and lecturer. As one of the early members of the Findhorn Community in Scotland, she was guided to tune into and harmonize with nature forces. She continues her work with nature beings at the Lorian Community in Canada.

One misconception about people who work with devas is that they are anti-technology and in general turn their backs on the modern world. In her essay "Human and Angels Now," however, Maclean explains that there is nothing wrong with modern technology, but rather the problem is in the way technology is applied. She also writes about the possibility of cooperation between humans and devas at the present time in our human evolution:

> The devas can also provide conscious cooperation with humans who seek their aid from holistic motives. They will cooperate in annulling the destruction man has inflicted on the planet, as we play our part. They will cooperate in joint creative efforts to improve the plant life that they have already created, with hybrids and new experiments, as we play our part. They will cooperate with scientific ecologists in ways yet to be developed.

## TOWARD A NEW WORLDVIEW

Communing with nature and learning how to see the world from nature's point of view is part of a new philosophy known as *deep ecology*. It is an outgrowth of early native beliefs that the Earth is a living body and that "God" or the Great Spirit endowed all of nature with innate wisdom, a wisdom that we (as children of the Earth) also share. Deep ecology teaches that life is interconnected and interrelated on the most fundamental levels and that we must strive to listen to and understand the other voices of nature in order to better perceive the needs of our planetary home. As defined by Bill Devall and George Sessions, "Deep ecology goes beyond a limited piecemeal shallow approach to environmental problems and attempts to articulate a comprehensive religious and philosophical worldview. The foundations of deep ecology are the basic intuitions of experiencing of ourselves and Nature which comprise ecological consciousness."

The instinctual understanding of our early environment was far more powerful among our ancestors than it is with us at the present time. Their conscious dependency on trees, rivers, and animals for food, protection, healing, shelter, and other forms of sustenance led our early ancestors to possess a deep awareness of their environment. As a result, they also knew (as many so-called "primitive" people do today) how to play a benign yet active part in the natural world. Nature was embraced not as an adversary but as a benefactor, to be treated as a generous parent and friend. A Native American elder from the Northwest asks, "How could nature ever be angry with us when we get everything we have from nature—our food, material for our dwellings and clothing—everything given us by nature?"

Although we still understand intellectually that our movements are controlled by Earth's gravitational field, or that a woman's menstrual cycle responds to the phases of the Moon, for example, we are often not as aware of the role that geography, climate, humidity, light, and temperature may have on us both as individuals and as a society. Attention to the ongoing discoveries of modern science about the ecological importance of plants, rivers, air currents, and geological formations, together with an appreciation of the metaphysical aspect of nature reflected in folklore and anthropology, can help us achieve a new relationship of wonder, appreciation, respect, and gratitude toward the vast community of life in both our immediate surroundings and the larger bioregions that make up our planetary home. Our lost connection with Earth wisdom and compassion can be achieved on a practical, everyday level. Through seeking to commune with our "relatives" on the biosphere's subtle planes, we embark on an exciting journey of discovery, alignment, and healing.

# 3
# Keynotes to Communication

*The art of integrated living consists in the spirit of intelligent cooperation between nature and spirit. Nature is blind without spirit; spirit is lame without nature. . . . Nature and spirit—by virtue of their purposeful togetherness—can make life gloriously meaningful.*
**—Haridas Chauduri, Mastering the Problems of Living**

During the summer of 1971, I had the privilege of meeting Geoffrey Hodson at the annual convention of The Theosophical Society in America. A clairvoyant and healer, he was the author of more than thirty books, including two classics about the devic hierarchy, *The Brotherhood of Angels and of Men* and *The Kingdom of the Gods.* The latter book contained not only descriptions of different nature spirits Hodson had observed, but also color drawings of devas as described by him to a professional artist.

I was both awestruck and intimidated by this imposing yet kindly English gentleman. Even at the age of eighty-five, he was filled with energy, and his blue eyes were both penetrating and observant. As he greeted me, I thought that he was clairvoyantly assessing the degree of my spiritual evolution, while taking note of my many faults and failures.

While I yearned to communicate with devas as Hodson had, I created a number of mental blocks that held me back from such exploration for many years:

First, I assumed that I needed to be highly evolved spiritually. I interpreted this as being free of personal faults and conflicts, as well as having the gift of clairvoyant perception.

Aware of the vast destruction that the human race has done to nature, I felt guilty about contributing to this destruction. I believed that nature spirits must be angry at us, and I felt uncomfortable about trying to communicate with them.

Finally, I didn't know what to do with a deva or nature spirit if I met one. Being a rather pragmatic young man just out of college, I could not see how communicating with devas would benefit me on a practical, everyday level. It was not until I finally began working with devas in 1990, after my experience in the Montréal Botanical Garden, that I received clear answers to each of my concerns.

## THE DOORS ARE OPEN

The first thing I realized, as I reflected on my sudden and instinctive impulse to ask a tree for help, was that communicating with nature spirits is part of our human heritage. I also understood that it wasn't that the devas were not interested in communicating with me, but rather that I had blocked myself from reaching out to *them*. Much had to do with my own limited perspectives about myself as a human being: about what I was able to accomplish and what my place was in the natural world. I had adhered to the widespread belief that I was both separate and autonomous from nature, and I had tended to see the nonanimal world as one made up of objects—not as a world of living beings to whom I was intimately connected.

I realized that one does not need to be a clairvoyant like Geoffrey Hodson to commune with nature spirits. Although feeling love for nature and cultivating a degree of sensitivity toward the natural world is an essential requirement, idealistically believing that I needed to be clairvoyant was actually blocking me from valuable contact with the nature beings. By learning to observe nature, we can gradually develop the "fine-tuning" necessary for human-deva communication.

Throughout human history, devas have communicated in many different ways, with a wide variety of individuals from a multitude of backgrounds, degrees of spiritual knowledge, and varying levels of consciousness. Four factors can help facilitate this communion:

1. Having a genuine interest in working with nature spirits from a perspective that goes beyond ego-gratification.

2. Approaching nature with feelings of wonder, curiosity, and respect.

3. Being open to the energetic, psychological, mental, and spiritual possibilities that communication with nature spirits can bring about.

4. Cultivating an awareness of and sensitivity toward the natural world that enables us to "tune in" to devic energies.

Communicating with nature beings increases *direct, firsthand participation* in the natural world with the goals of both helping to protect the environment and furthering the evolution of life. As we increase our understanding of the needs of the natural world, we become more effective as "planetary stewards," assisting the devas in their creative work. At a time when the threats to the natural environment are greater than at any time in human history, the need for such a unified effort is crucial. The devas are painfully aware of the need for all living beings to work together to help heal our planetary home, and they are more open to working with us than ever before.

Communion with nature spirits is vital to us as individuals for dozens of reasons, but four major themes stand out: becoming "grounded," accessing Earth wisdom, expanding our perspectives as human beings, and achieving "alignment."

# GROUNDEDNESS

In earlier times, when human beings lived much more as a part of their natural environment, this contact with the land produced a state of "groundedness," a state of fusion with the earth on physical, emotional, mental, and spiritual levels. As a result of being grounded, individuals enjoyed a state of harmony with nature and the strong sense of inner security this brings. According to Native American tradition, this groundedness brought about sensitivity to one's natural surroundings and enabled tribal members to "walk gently" on the Earth Mother. Groundedness was also seen as an essential prerequisite to open one up to the Greater Mysteries and the possibility of mystical learning experiences, considered the only way to grasp certain intangible laws of the universe. For Native Americans, the land was not only a source of food and shelter, but also a place to gather wisdom and receive inspiration.

Among the Australian aboriginals, every mountain, spring, animal, and rock is believed to possess its own animating spirit as created by ancestral consciousness common to all living beings. Earth-centered initiation rites allow the Aborigines to increase instinctual awareness of Earth rhythms and Earth energy. According to Robert Lawlor in *Voices of the First Day*, participants devote many hours to ceremonial chanting during these sacred rites, which allows them to enter expanded states of consciousness that resonate with the Earth's magnetic vibration.

Being grounded in nature was also emphasized by the Druids through their seasonal festivals. Alban Altane, the winter solstice, celebrated the rebirth of the Sun from the Great Mother, while Alban Hervin, the summer solstice, acknowledged "Father" Sun's achievement in reaching the highest point of the heavenly realms. Celebrating the spring and autumn equinoxes (Alban Eiler and Alban Elved, respectively) empha-sized reaping and harvesting of the Earth's generous gifts. Beltane (May 1) celebrated the magic of the blossoming Earth, while Samhuinn (Hal-loween) acknowledged what Druid Ross Nichols calls "the magic of death of time" and the open doors between the worlds of the living and the dead. Unlike modern religious festivals, which often take place indoors, the Druids' ceremonies were held primarily in sacred groves and forest clearings, where participants could fully experience the full pres-ence of the elements.

Writing in *ReVISION* magazine, Dr. Willis Harman, president of the Institute for Noetic Sciences, speaks of our ancestral tradition of com-munion and participation with the natural world:

> For a person living in the medieval world (as in many traditional societies), life is a seamless whole. Rocks, trees, rivers, and clouds are wondrous and alive; the world is enchanted, infused with spirit. Human beings feel at home in nature; the cosmos is a place of *belonging*. . . . The universe is alive and imbued with purpose; all creatures are part of a Great Chain of Being, with man between the angels and lower ani-mals. The working of enchantments, the occurrence of miracles, the presence of . . . beings with supernatural powers are—if not common-place—assumed to be quite real and consequential.

Sadly, much of modern humanity has lost this enchantment. As human beings became more civilized, we moved farther and farther away from the land. We settled in cities and towns where the environment is often artificially controlled in a variety of ways. Even in rural areas there is still a degree of detachment from the natural world; electricity, air conditioning, cable television, herbicides, lawn mowers, automobiles, and telephones are facts of modern civilization everywhere.

Cutting ourselves off from the land has led to a state that body-oriented psychotherapists like Alexander Lowen, the founder of Bioenergetics, call "ungroundedness." In addition to feeling disconnected from the land, we have also become cut off from our innate "animal" consciousness, which can deprive us of the wisdom and inner security we may have experienced in generations past. The result of this ungrounded state is often insecurity and fear, which leads in turn—as a vicious cycle—toward a certain degree of indifference to the natural world around us. Over the years, nature has been viewed more as an adversary to be feared, defended against, controlled, exploited, and abused. Rather than being regarded as a benign, nurturing mother, the Earth is treated as an economic commodity to do with as we wish.

When we as a society lose our grounding, our collective energy often moves from a heart-centered place of compassion toward the cold calculations of the rational mind. This rational approach to life can trap us (both individually and collectively) in compulsive patterns of greed, status seeking, indifference toward others, and competition as we try to find substitutes for the security we have lost by not being grounded. Feelings of pride and superiority over other living beings, the desire to control and dominate others, addiction to greed, and the quest for "appearance values" like status and prestige can be traced to being physically and psychologically ungrounded. Not only has this attitude led to the relentless accumulation of material goods in pursuit of security, but it has also led to a disregard and even contempt toward the other living beings that make up the rest of the natural world. The large-scale destruction of forests, acid rain, air and water pollution, and toxic waste dumps are among the more obvious examples of humanity's disregard toward the natural world.

As we become aware of both the complexity and the extent of the ecological catastrophe that is threatening our living planet, many of us become even more numb, as though to insulate ourselves from the pain and hopelessness that we feel. This is a very understandable reaction, not unlike that of a cancer patient being told that he or she has a terminal illness. Yet as the result of this psychic numbing, we tend to limit our participation in the world even more than before, perhaps because we feel powerless to change the situation. Ironically, by doing this, we continue to give our personal power away to the very individuals (such

*Cypress, Monterey, California*

as politicians, industrialists, and other decision-makers) who either set public policy or are actively involved in the systematic destruction of our planetary home in the first place.

In spite of tremendous threats to our survival, there is still much cause for optimism and hope. The immense power of the Earth to support life, the self-healing qualities of nature, and the vast untapped potential of humans to create change in the world are greatly underestimated by the vast majority of us. When we come into greater contact with nature, we are able to intuitively perceive the more subtle and unseen powers that stand behind material existence. At the same time, we gain a deeper understanding of our own creative potential as participants in the Earth's evolutionary journey.

Because they are intimately connected to earthly forms, nature spirits can help us reclaim our innate groundedness to the Earth. One way to achieve this state is to simply feel the Earth: take off our shoes and stand on the ground, and imagine ourselves being "anchored" into it. We can also sit or lie on the ground, stamp our feet, or do whatever else helps us to feel the Earth beneath us. (Other exercises and visualizations to increase groundedness are included in Part 3.)

At the same time, we can open ourselves to experience the reality of connectedness with the Earth Mother, and see ourselves as part of her rather than as a being who stands apart as a separate entity. Many of us—especially those of us who live in large cities—have been ungrounded for years. Reclaiming our innate capacity to be grounded may take time and involve repeated contact with the Earth on a regular, ongoing basis.

In the book *Finding Your Personal Power Spots*, José Alberto Rosa deals extensively with the subject of groundedness. Rosa, a psychiatrist who has worked in bioenergetic therapy for many years, includes numerous self-help exercises that have enabled his clients and workshop participants to achieve a greater sense of physical and energetic groundedness when working in their power spots. In a discussion on the importance of groundedness as the foundation for self-transformation, he stresses:

> Only by coming back to the land, by respecting the Earth Mother and by making peace with Her can we break the dangerous vicious cycles which threaten our existence. By becoming truly grounded we are able (both individually and collectively) to transform our society, which is in a state of crisis and disrepair. We can then create new, more natural ways of living that are in harmony with the earth, and which will lead to greater security and balance.

## GAINING WISDOM FROM EARTH ENERGY

Energy permeates the entire universe. Energies and forces are pouring upon our planet potently and ceaselessly and have been behind the cycle of creation since the beginning of time. Energy permeates everything in nature and animates all life on Earth. This life energy has different names. The ancient Chinese called it *chi*, while Jewish esoteric teachings refer to the life force as *chai*. *Chiatanya* means life force in Sanskrit. The noted biochemist Rupert Sheldrake describes the nature of this vital force in *The Rebirth of Nature*:

> Energy is indeed present in all living things. Living organisms draw it from their environment, as plants take it from the sun in photosynthesis and animals take chemical energy from their food through digestion and respiration. They accumulate it in their own bodies and use it to power their movements and behavior. When they die, the energy accumulated in their bodies is released to continue on its way in other forms. The flow of energy on which your body and your brain depend at this very

moment is part of the cosmic flux, and the energy within you will flow on after you are dead and gone, taking endless new forms.

This vital force acts on the air we breathe, the food we eat, and creates and sustains living tissue. It is present through the entire natural world. This is why many of us feel revitalized after a dip in the ocean, a walk in the woods, or a picnic on a lawn or open field. Chi masters often advise their students to go to the forest in order to access chi for achieving healing, inner focus, and self-empowerment.

Human beings have a unique role regarding energy. In addition to learning how to channel and focus our own personal energy (manifested by our emotions, thoughts, and deeds), we also have a responsibility to utilize planetary energy to aid in the evolution of all life. Because energy can be used in both benign and malevolent ways, we need to understand its power and learn how to channel it in safe directions that promote healing, unity, and growth.

Energy itself is a powerful yet neutral force that takes on a different vibration, tenor, character, and strength according to the life forms that are associated with it. For example, the energy from a waterfall feels different than the energy from a tree, just as the energy from an ancient redwood feels different from that of a redwood sapling. We also know that each person's energy differs from that of another, while the same person's energy can vary according to mood, thoughts, and physical state. Throughout the day, we constantly perceive different kinds of energies from our natural environment. At the same time, the energies that emanate from us help create the natural environment as well.

Love, for example, is a form of energy that exists at a certain vibration. We instinctively recognize when someone shares their love with us, even if they are standing across a room. Wisdom is another type of energy that one can perceive. Some of us have sat before a teacher, guru, or other spiritual leader and felt strong emanations of wisdom from them, even when they were not speaking.

Energies take on different strengths in nature as well. Many of us who have visited "planetary power spots" like Niagara Falls, the Grand Canyon, Ayers Rock, or Mont Blanc have sensed a tremendous power emanating around them. By the same token, a large parking lot, a garbage dump, or a war-torn landscape often feels "dead" to us, as though it were completely devoid of energy. Generally speaking, devas tend to be present where there is life: The greater the energy around the natural form, the greater the devic presence.

Members of the devic hierarchy are potent sources of Earth wisdom. By learning how to receive their energy, we are able to access the wisdom that they have to share with us. This wisdom will enable us to become more responsible, more caring, and wiser members of our community. In fact, devas may be able to assist us with all areas of understanding, since they are in direct contact with all of the wisdom that resides in and around the Earth.

Humans possess a vast untapped storehouse of innate natural wisdom. Shamans and medicine people in indigenous cultures are often considered to be living libraries of natural wisdom, because they have tapped their innate potential as guides and healers. Don Juan and Don Genaro of the Carlos Castaneda books, the Oglala Sioux medicine man Black Elk, Lynn Andrews, and Medicine Grizzlybear are some of the best-known shamans in the West. Most people experience life through the filters and perspectives of others, but these wisdom healers experience life directly through firsthand experience with nature. By striving to experience nature directly, we, too, can tap our innate potential as wise and compassionate human beings.

## EXPANDING OUR PERSPECTIVES

Energetic resonance with nature allows us to appreciate the interrelatedness of the natural world, of how the welfare of one living being depends on the welfare of the others. We realize that we are a part of the planetary picture, and we begin to appreciate the impact that humans have on the rest of the natural world.

In the *Mono Lake Guidebook*, environmentalist Gray Brechin speaks of the possibility of a powerful "place spirit" existing at Mono Lake in California, and he expresses both his appreciation of the spirit and concern for the lake's survival:

> Whether Mono Lake has a consciousness will remain one of its mysteries. But Mono endows its friends with awareness, for we have all had to learn from it. Mono has taught us to see the world anew, to accept and perceive beauties we had been unaware of, and to ask questions whose answers may be far from simple or comfortable. On the solitude of its beaches, at dawn and at dusk, we have learned to listen and to watch and to live quietly with ourselves. But mostly, we have learned to live with other beings which we cannot use but whose mere

presence enhances our daily existence. Mono doesn't ask simple questions. It demands an examination of the inner and outer worlds which constitute human awareness. And that is why it is the best kind of friend, and that is why we cannot let it die.

As we begin to yearn for a deeper connection to the Earth and the other living beings with whom we share this planet, this, in turn, stimulates our innate curiosity as human beings. It ignites the desire to learn more about our planet and its varied living systems, to gain a clearer understanding of the relationship between the winds and the birds, the rains, the soil and the plants, the animals and the trees—not just from an intellectual level, but from a perspective of wanting to know more about the life of a dear, long-lost friend. Inspired to protect, preserve, and further the life of this friend, we may want to read books and take classes on subjects like biology, geology, and botany; we may also undertake direct learning, by studying nature's physical forms and by communing with the subtle beings in nature that are connected to lakes, rocks, winds, or trees.

At a point in our evolution when the Earth is severely threatened by environmental destruction, the devas, deeply connected to Earth rhythms and Earth wisdom, are *the* beings to consult in our efforts to understand how we can most effectively work to help protect the waters, fields, forests, and air. Although we are numerically a very small part of the world community, we have developed a technological potential that goes far beyond our numbers. This unique power, which can either destroy our planetary home or can be used to help save it, should increase our feeling of personal responsibility toward the planet and all her inhabitants. The devas understand that all life is interdependent and interconnected, that the destruction of even a single species of animal or plant diminishes the integrity of the rest of creation. One of their tasks is to help us expand our perspectives on life and our role as responsible planetary citizens.

## ALIGNMENT

Through an expanded level of perception, we gradually become more aware of ourselves as human beings and of the world in which we live. This awareness enables us to align our energies on mental, emotional, physical, and energetic levels. This alignment—which extends to our deepest being—will increase our mental focus, emotional sensitivity and physical power. These qualities are needed to become active Earth healers. Alignment brings about a number of important benefits:

1. A sense of connectedness to our natural selves, as well as to the trees, the waters, the winds, and other animals. We realize through caring for other life forms as though they were members of our immediate family that what is good for the *whole* is good for us.

2. We gain a deeper knowledge of the overall movement of life and gain a firsthand understanding of the needs of other life forms that goes beyond the teaching of books, classroom lectures, and religious doctrine.

3. We break through old mental conditioning, illusions, and projections so that we can more effectively work to protect the planet. At the same time, we discover our personal task in life, a goal that is often illusive to most of us.

4. Through the ongoing alignment both within our beings and with the rest of the natural world, we gradually become empowered. We become strong yet sensitive, confident yet humble, active yet receptive, courageous and gentle.

The quest for alignment and connectedness is not always an easy journey. It involves relinquishing many cherished beliefs that we will find no longer useful. It may involve coming to terms with old wounds that might have created these beliefs in the first place. Many times, this inner work makes us feel vulnerable and afraid. By being open to the powers inherent in nature, however—powers that are also inherent within ourselves—this journey can be an exciting adventure of discovery that can continue throughout our lives.

PART TWO

# STEPS
# TO
# RECEPTIVITY

# 4
# Acknowledgment

*The finest workers in stone are not copper or steel tools,*
*but the gentle touches of air and water working at their leisure*
*with a liberal allowance of time.*
**—Henry David Thoreau**

An awareness and appreciation of nature are primary components of working with nature spirits. Without these, it is difficult for communication to take place.

Many early cultures enjoyed a deep connectedness with nature, and early traditions have continued to this day. In China, terrestrial astrology was developed during the Han dynasty in the second century A.D. By skillful surveying and by interpreting land forms like hills, rocks, trees, and springs, astrologers and geomancers were able to assist the imperial families in establishing their palaces and temples in places where they would best harmonize with what they called "cosmic breath," bringing the inhabitants health, prosperity, and good fortune. Many of the sacred temples, gardens, palaces, and tombs found in East Asia today thus were located and built in harmony with the subtle energies of the landscape.

The modern art and science of *feng-shui* evolved from this tradition. In many parts of East Asia today—including modern cities like Hong Kong, Taipei, and Singapore—practitioners of feng-shui are in great demand by home builders, restaurant owners, and developers of office buildings to help them locate their buildings in harmony with the natural environment.

Like our early human ancestors, many indigenous peoples in the world today possess a deep awareness of nature. In the Caquetá River basin in the Colombian Amazon, for example, hunters of the Miraña communities are able to detect an animal's presence at a distance of forty feet through their highly developed sense of smell. Like other Amazonian peoples, the Mirana believe that their entire world is populated by spirits, and they humbly ask permission of the spirits before they hunt or fish for game and when they plant and harvest trees, vegetables, and fruits. Like the Shuar of Ecuador and the Machiguenga of Peru, Miraña shamans make extensive use of ayahuasca (made primarily from the sacred psychotropic plant *Banisteriopsis caapi*) to enable them to enter the subtle realms of the forest spirits for healing and guidance.

Language is often a reflection of the degree of a culture's awareness of nature. Few languages enjoy the richness and complexity of those of the Australian aboriginals in their focus on natural life. According to Robert Lawlor in *Voices of the First Day,* "Aboriginal dialects have hundreds of names for each particular type of tree, and they have names for many individual trees. In the case of fish and animals, there are sometimes separate names for the same fish or animal at different stages of its breeding cycle." Some aboriginal languages have forty to fifty terms to signify different shapes of leaves and specific terms for the Sun at each hour of the day. By the same token, the vocabulary of the Inuit of the Arctic Circle contains literally dozens of different terms for the English word "snow." This focus on nature is typical of many other native societies in North America as well. Ernest Benedict, a Mohawk elder, says in *Respect for Nature:*

> Our people see that things of nature are given high priority, because the things of nature can exist without man but man cannot exist without nature. If white people harbored this spirit of gratitude for the gifts of nature, the earth would become a better place in which to live, because you do not destroy what you cherish and revere.

Few of us who live in the industrialized nations of the world can claim to have the awareness toward and appreciation of the natural world that is shown by many indigenous peoples. Many of us spend our lives in air-conditioned homes, ride in air-conditioned cars, and work or study in climate-controlled businesses and schools. We often dull our senses with highly processed foods that are rich in salt and artificial flavorings, and eat tasteless "fresh" foods that have taken weeks to arrive in the market from the time they are harvested. Even when we are outdoors, we are either subjected to traffic or city noises or are distracted by the sounds of radios or tape players. Little wonder so few of us enjoy the opportunity to develop our innate senses of hearing, smell, touch, and sight.

# INTUITIONAL PERCEPTION

Developing our five acknowledged senses—sight, hearing, smell, taste, and touch—is essential if we yearn to commune with nature's subtle forces. It is not unlike needing to have a sensitive antenna and other electrical equipment if we want to receive television transmissions. If the station emits a given frequency, our antenna needs to resonate with this frequency or our television set will be blank. By the same token, sensitivity is necessary for us to resonate with the energies transmitted by the members of the subtle realms.

One natural expansion of the basic five senses is the most important "sense" of all: the intuition. Intuition is often called "the mind's eye" of perception because it enables us to perceive that something is true although it may not be directly confirmed by previous intellectual knowledge or information. It is "knowing" that transcends space and time and brings us to direct, firsthand understanding. In *Glamour: A World Problem*, Alice Bailey defines intuition in the following way:

> Intuition is a comprehensive grip of the principle of universality, and when it is functioning there is, momentarily at least, a complete loss of the sense of separateness. At its highest point, it is known as that Universal Love which has no relation to sentiment . . . but is, predominantly, in the nature of identification with all beings.

All of us possess a degree of intuition; however, many of us are not aware of its presence, while those of us who are often do not trust it. In a world where we are bombarded from all sides with external stimuli—as well as with our own desires and mental projections—intuition is an essential tool to help us see reality. Advertising, political rhetoric, religious injunction, and other forms of conditioning from parents, organized religion, coworkers, and teachers often leave us challenged to focus within and come upon an understanding of an issue that is based on our intuitive perception.

Becoming grounded is an essential component of developing intuition, because it brings about alignment with both the Earth and with our natural, instinctual selves. Through groundedness we learn how to listen with our hearts as opposed to with the mind alone; we learn how to view life from a heart-centered perspective.

Cultivating the qualities of discrimination and dispassion is also essential for developing the intuition. In a society where glamour, outer appearance, and illusion are often accepted as reality, we need to be able to discern between the false and the true, and between form and the reality behind the form. Through dispassion, we are able to view an issue in its proper perspective without becoming entrapped by its drama. Asking ourselves "What is the truth here?" and seeking to be open by not judging, we are able to contact our inner wisdom. By striving to use our innate faculties of discrimination and dispassion in daily life, we can gradually learn how to view a statement or a situation in a larger context free from preconceived ideas or expected outcomes. We are able to perceive acts in their true perspective and their proper significance.

Meditation is an essential key to developing the intuition. Many religious traditions—including Buddhist, Hindu, Sufi and Christian—have spoken of the value of meditation whose goal is to erase the thinking mind of its desires, projections, evaluation, and judgments. As the mind becomes more relaxed, the intuition can begin to make itself felt. There are, of course, many different methods of meditation. (One meditation exercise is included in chapter 8, "Invocation," although it may not be appropriate for everyone.) Whatever method you choose, try to use meditation as a way to develop alignment and a deeper relationship within all aspects of your being. Eventually, you will become more sensitive to your intuitive powers and more open to communication with the devic realms.

In *The Kingdom of the Gods*, Geoffrey Hodson observes: "Angels . . . see thought processes, emotions and aspirations as external and material phenomena; for they live in the worlds of feeling, thought, spiritual intuition and spiritual will." Because members of the devic realms function at a high level of intuition and primarily perceive life in terms of energies, they communicate through life's higher frequency. By opening ourselves to our own intuition, we are better able to receive the wisdom, inspiration, and love the devas have to share with us.

# VISITING NATURE

The first step toward acknowledging nature involves going to a place of natural beauty. The location is up to you. It may be the flower bed in your backyard; it may be your favorite spot on a beach, in a park, or in a botanical garden. You may wish to take a walk in the woods or visit a spot in the wilderness to which you are very attracted.

Although you may have visited this special place many times before, there are several guidelines to remember in the context of your work:

1. Have a flexible timetable. Make sure that you have adequate time to spend several hours on your visit, which should be for as long as you feel comfortable. If possible, leave your watch at home.
2. Approach the place you are visiting with a spirit of friendliness and silent receptivity. Devas do not generally respond well to loud, sudden noises. They are often afraid of humans, who are the primary destroyers of the devas' natural world. So walk softly and gently.
3. Relax and "settle in." Take the time to become aware of the tremendous variety of living beings in the area: the larger and smaller plants, the flying and creeping insects, the birds and other mammals, the rocks, the waves and other natural forms.
4. Strive to use as many senses as possible. Smell the flower. Touch the tree. Listen to the insects, the birds, and the wind. Allow the water to run through your fingers. Take the time to carefully observe the life around you. Place your focus on what attracts your attention and allow your innate curiosity to guide your observation. If you are looking at a tree, examine it carefully, from the roots to the leaves. Observe how it moves in the wind. See the rustle of the leaves and the texture of the bark. Observe the shape of the branches and the leaves. Remember that using your sense of sight does not need to involve thinking, evaluating, or analyzing. It involves simple visual observation. Now close your eyes and use your other senses to learn more. Listen to the rustle of the leaves. Touch the trunk and branches and feel the texture of the bark. Press your nose against the tree and smell the bark. Lean against the tree and feel its energetic presence.

An interesting variation would be to take a "blind walk," best taken with a trusted friend or family member. In this type of walk, you are blindfolded. Before you begin, turn around several times so that you lose your sense of direction. Then allow your friend to lead you to a natural

*Lion Waterfall, near Pucón, Chile*

form (such as a tree, bush, rock, or water source). You can then get to know this form through touch, hearing, and smell.

Another activity involves simply going to a place of your choice (such as a patch of grass among taller plants, a clearing by a stream, or a clearing surrounded by trees). Lie down comfortably on your back and look up at the sky. As you take some deep, relaxing breaths, strive to feel as though you are actually merging or becoming what you are lying upon. Listen to the sounds. You may also want to close your eyes and use other senses to commune with your environment. Some of these activities will help lay the groundwork for devic invocation and communion described in chapters 8 and 9.

## THE ROLE OF BEAUTY

Throughout human history, beauty has been an essential component in spiritual understanding. To the Navajo, for example, beauty has always been recognized as the culmination of the subtle intelligent life of the universe. Natural phenomena—like mountains, canyons, rivers, lakes, and rock formations—are all considered to be the homes of powerful spirit beings. Many of the Navajo's most sacred sites—such as Spider Rock in Canyon de Chelly in northern New Mexico, believed to be the earthly abode of the rainbow-weaving Spider Grandmother—are among the most beautiful natural places in North America.

Being alert to the beauty of nature enables us to acknowledge and appreciate nature to the fullest. Not only does beauty allow us to see the magical radiance of the form itself, but it inspires us to become open to the wisdom and love that created the natural form. Coming upon the beauty of a flower, a tree, or a mountain often brings out our own most beautiful human qualities, including those of wonder, joy, and love.

Waterfalls have a special ability to enable us to appreciate beauty in all its dimensions. I learned from a deva connected to the powerful Dingman's Falls in eastern Pennsylvania how the impact of the deva's physical beauty and spiritual presence can help us dissolve old mental and emotional patterns and allow us to experience the timelessness of the "now moment." By observing a waterfall with attention to both the falls as a whole and the myriad small details (such as the dragonflies playing at the foot of the fall's cascade), we can open ourselves to the transformative aspects of its beauty and see nature and life in both a deeper and more expanded perspective.

*Trumpet Creepers, Brooklyn, New York*

In *The World Is As You Dream It*, a book about his experiences with the Shuar people of Ecuador, John Perkins writes movingly of the transformative beauty of a waterfall:

> The sacred waterfall of the Shuar is breathtaking and beautiful. Yet standing before it, looking up into the rainbow that arches through the cascading waters, the visitor is struck by a feeling that transcends the magnificence of the landscape. No matter what your religion, you cannot help but sense the spirit of this place. Its power defies any attempt to describe the euphoria inspired by a natural phenomenon so overwhelmingly grand that its voice seems to cross all the bridges of time, speaking to us from some ancient past as well as from the unknown future.

The beauty of natural forms can have a powerful impact on the work of artists and sculptors. For example, when an artist paints a picture of a lake after allowing herself to be open to its outer and inner beauty, the painting takes on a deeper quality, a more complex dimension. In other words, the artist is creating a work of art on many different levels of her being rather than being limited to artistic skill or intellectual sense of proportion.

## WORKING WITH FLOWERS

Exploring the world of flowers is one of the easiest and most enjoyable ways to help deepen our contact with the natural world and achieve a greater appreciation of nature. Although flowers have played a significant role in spiritual practice for tens of thousands of years, they are often unappreciated and underutilized as powerful agents in facilitating spiritual unfoldment. They can play a major role as a "portal of entry" in bringing us into the world of nature spirits. The conscious use of Bach Flower Remedies and other flower essences are believed to enable us to align the subtle emotional and mental aspects of our beings with the devic consciousness that guides the flowers' evolution. By ingesting the flower essence, we intimately partake of the devas' energy.

Why flowers? Flowers are one of nature's masterpieces that have much to offer on many levels:

1. Flowers are the ultimate expression of beauty. The flower is often the "focal" point of a plant or flowering tree, and serves to attract other living beings to the plant through visual beauty, color, and

aroma. It is vital for the plant's reproduction. In some plant species, such as certain varieties of bamboo, the flower is the final goal in the plant's individual evolution; after the flower blooms, the plant will die. Flowers offer incredible visual beauty through their myriad colors and forms, they come in a wide variety of shapes and sizes, and they emit hundreds of different fragrances, from the most subtle to the overpowering.

2. Flowers are nonthreatening and friendly. Everyone—no matter what age or cultural background—is attracted to at least some types of flowers.

3. Flowers offer a combination of both delicacy and strength; some survive and thrive in even the most difficult growing conditions. They serve as an example to help us balance the masculine and feminine aspects of our nature, which is an essential aspect of laying the groundwork for human-deva cooperation.

4. Different flowers appeal to different tastes. Some people relate best to a simple batch of daisies growing in an empty lot, while others feel inspired by an elegant clematis spreading its vines along a formal garden trellis.

5. Since they are rooted in the Earth Mother, the nature spirits connected to flowers offer both groundedness and Earth wisdom. Because flowers are everywhere, they are easily accessible, whether one lives in a large city or an isolated rural area.

One of the most appealing qualities of flowers is their ability to express themselves. By their very essence, they can offer us many important teachings about a wide variety of qualities, including gentleness, strength, passion, the lust for life, adaptability, expressiveness, grace, courage, fragility, and an unrestrained sense of giving.

In my early work with nature spirits, I would often visit flowers throughout the borough of Brooklyn, New York, intent on receiving what they had to share with me. One of my discoveries was that the flowers often reflect the needs of the human beings in their immediate environment. For example, flowers planted outside a school play a role in influencing the students who pass them on the way to class, while a flower planted near a tree often has a teaching role that is somehow connected to that of the tree. One day I visited a group of field bindweed, growing around a fire hydrant in an abandoned lot in Red Hook, one of Brooklyn's toughest and most depressing neighborhoods. Although I did not know it at the time, this vacant lot was a gathering place for drug addicts and prostitutes after dark.

The message that I received from the bindweed spirit moved me deeply. It told of how flowers offer us hope to help us transcend our human difficulties. Through a potent combination of beauty, color, aroma, and spiritual energy, flowers "break through" our outer psychological armoring and make contact with our higher nature, where inspiration and wisdom reside. Their energy touches and awakens the tiny spark of hope that lies within each of us, leading to transformation in even the most dispirited and depressed individual. The bindweed spirit invited me to visit flowers in gardens, parks, fields, roadsides and even in empty lots, for spiritual awakening and transformation.

Which are the best flowers to visit? Much depends on personal taste and how we feel at the moment. Although all flowers that are connected to the Earth Mother can offer earthly wisdom, I have found that the most interesting flowers are those that grow wild, in the fields, in the woods, by the roadside and in vacant lots. The messages from highly cultivated and well-tended flowers in places like a formal garden may contain inspiring spiritual messages, while flowers growing on their own in a field or an abandoned lot are more likely to provide basic, direct, "streetwise" information about survival, relationship, dignity, or ecological conscious-ness that would be of more practical value. Even the simplest flowers can offer spiritual insight. One of my favorites was communicated by a deva connected to a group of daisies growing by a city street. It spoke of its role as the portal of entry to the spirit realms that were accessible to all beings.

If you want to work with flower devas, visit flowers to which you feel intuitively drawn. If you are open and sensitive to them, flowers will silently "call out" to you and attract your attention.

The best way to approach flowers is from a place of friendliness, very much like you would approach a puppy or a kitten. Although you may wish to talk to them, this is not always necessary; they respond more to our energies than to what we may say to them. Observe the flower with an open heart, acknowledging its beauty, grace, and quiet strength. Be receptive and sensitive, for you are communing with a living work of art!

## GATHERING KNOWLEDGE

Direct contact with lakes, streams, trees, rocks, and flowers is essential for learning about nature, but reading books, going to classes, attending workshops, and viewing audiovisual programs can be a valuable comple-ment to firsthand experience. Many of us have read about the long treks

The daisy: "We are an accessible flower. We appeal to simple, straightforward tastes. . . . In a sense, we stand at the entry gate to the world of spiritual light. We do not sit at the throne of God, but outside the gates where you begin to experience the gifts of the spiritual world. We make you feel welcome, we make you feel glad that you are here—no matter how unworthy you feel, or how battered and tormented your life may be. By entering your consciousness, we tell you that you are worthy and welcome. And we offer a simple, caring, straightforward message: that of love, hope, and above all, acceptance."

and wilderness-living experience of the pioneer naturalist and environmentalist John Muir. Muir, who often spent months alone in the wilderness, is often viewed as essentially a mystic and a visionary. Yet he was also a scientist who brought dozens of measuring instruments and books on geology, biology, and glaciology with him whenever he went into the wilderness. The balance between intellectual knowledge gained from books and other forms of research and the firsthand knowledge gained from direct contact with the natural world provided Muir with a depth and breadth of understanding that was unrivaled in his time.

Unfortunately, traditional scientific investigation has focused on the old mechanistic model of existence developed by the French philosopher René Descartes. His "closed systems" model taught that the natural world is made up of the sum of its individual parts, and that these parts function more or less independently of each other. One element of the environment has no relationship to anything else, and matter (that is, whatever can be measured and predicted) is viewed as the only reality. Until recently, this idea was accepted as the dominant scientific model of investigation.

Recent discoveries in biology and quantum physics, however, have found that the natural world is essentially an *open system:* one of interdependence, interrelationship, cooperation, chaos, and change. This model teaches that the world is more than the sum of its parts and that there is an intangible force or life energy that connects us to all other life on this planet and the universe. The universe should actually be pictured, says physicist Fritjof Capra, "as one indivisible, dynamic whole whose parts are essentially interrelated. . . . Systems biology, like the "new physics," emphasizes relationships rather than isolated entities—it speaks to the complex web of dynamic relationships between outwardly different forms of life."

Rather than investigate the secrets of biology, chemistry, geology, or botany as a closed system of study, we can apply our investigations toward understanding the interrelationships involved in our subject of interest. By broadening our perspective, we are able to achieve a clearer idea of the total picture. For example, if we were to study the problem of river flooding, we could focus on the origin and dynamics of the river itself. Although this would be valuable, we also should study the condition of the surrounding soil and the effects that deforestation, farming, highway construction, and urbanization may have had on the river's inability to stay within its banks. We would also need to see the connection between river flooding and changing weather patterns brought about by other forms of environmental stress. By making these connections, we would be better able to develop intelligent, long-term strategies that would benefit all life forms in the bioregion.

We need not limit ourselves to scientific study alone. Learning about how humans have historically related to our subject enables us to obtain a deeper, more personal understanding. For example, let's imagine that we live in northern California and want to learn more about oak trees. Learning about their habitats, growth patterns, and means of reproduction are both valuable and interesting. But what about how humans have related to oak trees? Acorns were a major staple food for many indigenous peoples in northern California, who ground the acorns into flour and used them to make a variety of foods. The Shasta, Yurok, Mewok, Yuma, Paiute, and Chumash tribes are among those whose very existence depended on the acorn harvest, and many traded acorns with other tribes for different varieties of nuts, seeds, hides and other goods. The book *Oaks of California* relates that oak trees were so revered by the California Indians that men and women often took on names like "Sweet Acorn" and "Striped Acorn." The Ohlone and Maidu peoples based their calendars on the acorn harvest; the Maidu calendar referred to our month of April, for example, as Winuti ("black oak tassel") and September as Matmeni ("acorn bread").

An open-systems approach to studying the other beings in the natural world deepens our understanding of nature and our relationship to it. This leads us to acknowledge nature and become more sensitive to its life and needs.

# 5

# Respect

---

*To issue from the workshops of Nature a thing must be worthy of
Nature's loving care and most painstaking art. Should it not be worthy
of your respect, at least?*
**—Mikhail Naimy, The Book of Mirdad**

Respect is essential for establishing benign contact with the subtle forces of nature. On the one hand, respect engenders trust, affection, and a willingness to share on the part of the nature spirits. At the same time, it provides us with the foundation to be open to what nature has to share with us, whether it be in the form of healing, inspiration, or wisdom.

Books like Bill Devall and George Session's *Deep Ecology,* and John Seed's *Thinking Like a Mountain* challenge the view that human beings are the final measure of creation and state that we make up one part of the Earth's vast family. They teach that our arrogance and disrespect toward nature is endangering not only ourselves, but all of life. Deep ecology recognizes that a total transformation of consciousness toward both ourselves and our relationship with the Earth is necessary to protect its life-support systems.

One of the primary laws of deep ecology is that every living thing has a reason for being here, a mission to accomplish, and has been given a special function in the overall scheme of things. Deep ecology teaches that the Earth is *one body* and that every living thing is part of the whole. If this "body" is to survive, we must learn to respect it, and in turn strive to respect all forms of life with which we share our planetary home.

Indigenous societies like the Navajo, the Australian aboriginals, and the Shuar have always realized that their very survival depends on the Earth's generosity. The stream that gives them fresh water to drink and fish to eat, the trees that provide protection, shade, food, shelter, and medicine, the sky that brings the rains, and the land that grows the crops and provides the foundation upon which they walk are looked upon with appreciation, every single day. Private property is generally unknown in societies that acknowledge the natural world in this way, for how can you own something of which you are an integral part?

This sense of acknowledgment generates respect, which in turn lays the foundation for the community's every interaction with its environment. For example, members of the Laguna Pueblo tribe in what is now New Mexico have developed elaborate ceremonies to show respect to the Earth Mother whenever they hunt for food. Prayers are offered to Great Spirit before the hunters leave the community and after they arrive at the hunting ground. Tribute is also offered to the deer who will provide them with food and clothing. One Laguna Pueblo elder (in *Respect for Life*) offered the following description of what takes place among the hunter and his companions when a freshly killed deer is skinned:

> When he starts cutting into the animal, everyone asks the Creator for forgiveness for cutting into this carcass—for cutting into the meat of the deer and the skin as well. And when he cuts the heart, they ask the Creator for an abundance of deer in the future. . . . As soon as the deer has been cleaned, a small bed is made on the east side of an evergreen tree or a cedar, or whatever nearby is green, and everything from the deer's insides are placed on this soft bed. Prayers are offered once again and charm stones are laid. And any animal that may be served as a result of the luck is invited to enjoy its dinner.

Respect toward nature is also an essential component of the daily life of the Machiguenga in southeastern Peru. Like other Amazonian people, the physical and spiritual worlds of the Machiguenga are impossible to separate, and they believe that every river, lake, plant, and animal is a spirit being. When they plant manioc, a staple food, they pray to the manioc spirits so that the plant will grow strong and healthy. And when they harvest the manioc months later, they ask the spirit to release the plant from the soil. Visitors to their community in Manu National Park are impressed at how their unique farming methods involving crop rotation and biodiversity are able to rejuvenate the rainforest over a twenty-year period. The Machiguenga's respect for nature and their work with the nature spirits has allowed them to thrive as a culture for thousands of years.

Unfortunately, respect and gratitude toward nature rarely play a role in the actions of most members of the industrial societies. Trees, wild animals, lakes, and rivers are viewed primarily as "natural resources" to be dominated, controlled, and exploited for financial gain. The plundering of the land for oil and precious metals, the trapping of foxes and ermine for their pelts, the clear-cutting of the forests for wood, and the ever-increasing pollution of the water and air by motor vehicles and factories attest to a profound lack of respect for the Earth.

In *The Earthsteward's Handbook,* Danaan Parry and Lila Forest quote the anguished words of a Wintu holy woman comparing the Native American and Caucasian approaches to respect toward the Earth:

> The White People never cared for land or deer or bear. When we Indians kill meat, we eat it all up. When we dig roots we make little holes. When we build houses, we make little holes. When we burn grass for grasshoppers, we don't ruin things. We shake down acorns and pine nuts. We don't chop down the trees. We only use dead wood. But the White People plow up the ground, pull down the trees, kill everything. The trees say, "Don't, I am sore. Don't hurt me." But they chop it down and cut it up. . . . How can the spirit of the earth like the White Man? . . . Everywhere the White Man has touched it, it is sore.

## THE ROOTS OF RESPECT

What is respect? The term itself traces its roots to the Latin *respectus,* meaning "to look back at" and "to regard." Respect implies acknowledging that the *selfhood* of others—as well as their beliefs and feelings—are important. This attitude is then reflected in our behavior toward them. Respect also implies understanding the needs of others (whether the "other" is a person, a tree, an animal, or a river) so that they can express themselves in the fullest way possible, according to their innate potential. This may involve allowing a child to pursue his or her chosen career, permitting a tree to fulfill its natural lifespan, allowing a dolphin to live its life in the ocean rather than holding it captive in an aquarium, or not controlling a river's natural flow through dams and levees. It may involve refraining from picking flowers, or harvesting fruit only at the point of ripeness.

Few would disagree that lack of respect is widespread in our world today. People are discriminated against because of their race, religion, sexual orientation, and gender. Men do not respect women and often treat them as adornments and sex objects. Healers who engage in natural or alternative healing practices like herbalism are often persecuted by the organized medical establishment. Elders are often dismissed by the younger generation and spend their final years in loneliness and despair. Millions of neglected and abandoned pets are "put to sleep" every year by animal shelters.

Though often a very scarce commodity, respect is essential for creating and maintaining the fabric of community, which includes all living beings. At a seminar concerning the upbringing of Native American children years ago, the educator John Gardner stressed that

> [respect] lies at the very center of a person's relation with his fellow man, starting with the child's relation to his family. It lies at the center of man's relation to nature and to the Great Spirit above him. You show that respect is really at the bottom of discipline and authority; it's basic to every kind of learning as well as to the enjoyment of life.

Children learn respect primarily by example from parents, teachers, and older siblings. Respect in its fullest sense not only includes respecting other people and their needs, feelings, and rights, but it involves respecting ourselves: our physical body through proper diet and exercise, along with respect for our own physical needs, our feelings, and our spiritual essence. Self-respect also includes respecting the energy that animates our bodies and respecting the natural forces that created us and sustain us and that also created and sustain other living beings.

Native Americans and other indigenous peoples have much to teach us about respectfully living on the Earth Mother. They can especially teach us how to achieve a more instinctual relationship with other life forms. According to John Gardner in *Respect for Life:*

> We have to be clear about the fact that it is not enough simply to live next to nature. It depends *how* you live next to nature, *how* you study her. Here, too, the Indian can show the way. If it is only the brain and not the heart that is listening for nature's message, her deeper teachings will not be heard. Her mysteries will be stripped away by a cold manner of knowing.

Learning about Earth-centered religious and cultural traditions can help lay the groundwork for gaining respect for nature. Thanks to recent developments in media and computer sciences, information about other cultural and religious traditions has become more accessible than perhaps ever before in history. Books, videotapes, and CD-ROM technology allow almost anyone to experience other cultures, whether they are reading about traditional Shinto religious practices and viewing their sacred shrines, or "visiting" a rainforest culture like the Machiguenga through a sensitively produced video such as *Spirits of the Rainforest.*

It is also much easier to travel to remote areas than it was in the past, although we need to be very sensitive toward the the cultural traditions of those we wish to visit. Several years ago I visited an isolated community of Cuna off the coast of Panama to do research for a book about sacred trees. I had only the name of a Cuna on the island who had studied anthropology in Panama City. I arrived on the island in a dugout canoe before dawn, and, not wanting to awaken my contact person, I wandered around the island alone. Being the only non-Cuna on the island, I attracted a good deal of attention. I asked people who spoke Spanish about sacred trees and tree spirits, but no one seemed to know anything about them.

After finally meeting my contact, I asked him about the trees. He became visibly uncomfortable, and told me that the only person to speak with about such matters was the tribal chief, who was accessible through a *nele*, or a Cuna shaman. Asking other members of the community (including himself) about sacred matters before speaking with the chief was an act of disrespect to the entire community. Smiling, he told me that "our meeting never took place," and directed me to the home of one of the neles, who eventually secured an appointment with the chief. After an hour-long visit, the chief suggested that I speak with a young anthropology graduate who lived on the island, who happened to be my original contact person. He was now able to speak freely about the Cuna's sacred ways, and he verified much of what the chief had told me about sacred trees. While I was fortunate to obtain the information I needed, I realized how little I knew about Cuna culture before I arrived, and how insensitive I was toward their religious and social traditions.

An increasing variety of specialized travel guides and culturally sensitive tour programs are available that can offer both tools and access for visiting native cultures and sacred sites. Some organizations, like "Journeys into American Indian Territory" (see Resources), introduce small groups of visitors to selected communities and expose them to native culture and traditions to an extent not usually available to outsiders. In some cases, a visit can actually entail participating in a sweat lodge, or attending a potluck, ceremonial dance, powwow, or other traditional activity. Learning about traditional culture—whether it involves reading about Shinto shrines, hearing an audiotape of Umbanda ceremonial chants in honor of the orishas, or attending an Apache potlatch—can help us appreciate the common element of respect that these cultures have for the Earth Mother.

# THE HEART-ORIENTED APPROACH TO NATURE

Cultivating self-respect involves becoming more aware of the forces that also create and sustain all other forms of life. As noted in the previous chapters, a fundamental part of this understanding comes from deep and frequent contact with nature from a heart-oriented perspective as opposed to a head-oriented one.

Simply being in nature, whether it involves journeying quietly along a forest trail, walking in silence by a stream, sitting with our back against the trunk of a tree, observing the flowers, listening to the wind, hearing the birds singing on the tree branches, seeing the flight of the insects, feeling the Earth and the rocks under our feet, or lying down on the ground and seeing the sky above us all contribute to this gradual process of deepening respect and wonder.

As we become more intimate with nature, we begin to feel her energy and understand her rhythms. We respect the power, beauty, and wisdom that is inherent in nature and all of her myriad expressions.

We also begin to see the interrelatedness of life. We learn to respect the essential integrated aspects of a forest or a swamp and come to appreciate the interplay of elements and how they contribute to a complex yet synchronized living whole. Gradually, this understanding will lead to us to identify with this interplay of elements, and we begin to know that we are an essential part of it. We slowly reclaim our nearly forgotten link with the land and with the animals and plants.

This process does not come about by thinking about it. Coming upon the reality of the interconnectedness and interdependence of all beings often takes place gradually, as we become grounded enough and receptive enough to allow it to manifest in our consciousness. Eventually this realization enables us to see both ourself and nature in a completely different light.

The heart-oriented approach to nature allows us to experience a greater degree of identification with the natural world. Identification with nature is far more valuable and lasting than identification with one's culture, racial group, political ideas, social movements, or material possessions. It is not only more worthwhile, but far more *real*. When we identify with the natural world, we are identifying *with the reality behind the form*, rather than with man-made creations like racial superiority, social status, and religious differences. Of course, such a fundamental shift in consciousness does not always take place as a predictable sequence of events, since one's reactions to nature are not necessarily sequential and linear!

Yet as we begin to feel a sense of oneness with nature, we not only assume our true identity, but more deeply understand our place as part of the natural order of life. We begin to discard old images of self-hate, self-depreciation, and feelings of worthlessness. We realize that we have a right to be here on Earth, and we cease to feel insignificant and unworthy. We begin to see ourself as a powerful, beautiful, and essentially loving part of nature's family, and we come upon the threshold of seeing our potentially important role in assisting the cause of evolution by the sharing of our gifts. We more clearly appreciate the sanctity of life, not only of our own lives as individuals, but that of other living beings as well.

As we live our lives, this all-encompassing and powerful feeling of respect for ourselves and others will reveal itself in thousands of small actions that are based on awareness, love, and compassion. These thoughts and actions will lead, as in a spiral, toward a deeper appreciation of our essential worth. And this greater self-respect will enable us to teach the attitude of respect by example—as opposed to imposing rules and standards on ourselves and others.

## "GROWING CORN"

The Native American Medicine Man Sun Bear often said, "If your philosophy doesn't grow corn, I don't want to hear about it." Wise words. Attitudes and ideas only reveal their true worth when applied in daily life.

Respect toward the Earth Mother requires both sensitivity and a strong commitment to action. The way it is expressed is up to each of us according to the gifts we have to share. It may simply involve tending the flowers in one's flowerpot or garden, or making sure that our companion animal is treated with respect, love, and affection.

Some people may want to expand their caring to the larger community. For instance, a city dweller can "adopt" a tree on one's street, provide it with water when necessary, and make sure that it is protected from abuse. Walking through a local park with a garbage bag and filling it with bottles, cans, papers, and other discarded materials can be a satisfying and useful activity. Getting involved with (or establishing) a local "friends of the park" association, planting trees, starting an urban garden, or creating "vest pocket" parks in vacant lots are tangible ways of showing our respect to the Earth Mother. Others may want to support their local botanical garden or get involved with organizations that are dedicated to saving and protecting the environment on an international, national, or local scale.

Purchasing products that are "environmentally friendly" and buying only what is really necessary can do much to show our respect for the environment. Recycling paper, metal, glass, plastic, and organic waste reduces pressure on landfills and lessens the need for mining aluminum and cutting trees. Using public transportation as much as possible and riding a bicycle or walking instead of taking the car reduces environmental pollution and save energy.

Eating low on the food chain can be a very personal expression of respect for both other animals and the planet on which we live. Plant-based diets not only reduce the demand to kill animals for food, but actually use less plant and water resources than meat-oriented diets. The average American, for example, consumes nearly a ton of grain a year, although only 150 pounds are consumed directly as bread or cereal. The rest is consumed indirectly as grain for food animals. The traditional mixed diet popular in the United States requires 2,500 gallons of water per person per day (including water for irrigation, animal drinking water, and the large amount of water used to process meat), while a plant-based diet uses only 300 gallons. Plant-based diets also involve much less pollution than those containing meat because they eliminate the tremendous damage to the environment caused by feedlot runoff and the air and water pollution caused by slaughterhouses. By eating low on the food chain we walk lightly on the Earth Mother by reducing the amount of stress we cause to the environment.

# AWARENESS OF THE SMALLEST

Although respecting the environment in our daily routine is our most important task, we need to become aware of what some call the "minor details" of life. Awareness toward even the smallest and (to our eyes) least significant forms of life was taught by sages throughout history, because they believed that attention to the small details of life reflects a larger attitude. In the words of an anonymous Chinese poet:

> I love this little weed
> A sparkle of life I find in it.
> A little weed is growing upon the waist of a wall,
> Lovely and lively.
> I water it every day.
> It has the importance of living as it grows.

Among the Jains, a religious sect in India based on the doctrine of *ahimsa,* or nonviolence, a religious person is forbidden to dig into the ground without good reason, and is advised not to uproot trees, trample on lawns, or pluck leaves, flowers, or immature fruits from trees. Some Jain monks take their vows so seriously that they refuse to ride in motor vehicles for fear of killing people or animals and are extremely careful of the welfare of insects even when they walk along the street. According to the Jain text *Atma Tatva Vichar:*

> A monk has to be overscrupulous to avoid any injury to subtle or gross beings, while moving, talking, eating, drinking, rising, sitting or sleeping. This is why the monks maintain a broomstick with them. With the help of extremely soft tips of woollen threads of the broom, they gently remove any living insect which might crawl on the body, dress, or other utensils lest it might be injured.

Most of us would have difficulty leading the nonviolent life of a Jain monk. But Rick Day describes a very contemporary application of sensitivity and respect toward the Earth during the installation of a septic system at a spiritual community in the Catskill Mountains:

> We installed it without damaging the environment. We took up the grassy sod before digging. The limbs were tied out of the way. Ditches

were dug by hand so as not to damage the large tree roots. I liked this new way of working in harmony with surrounding life. It is the manifestation of all our love.

Life forms are constantly being destroyed in order to ensure the survival of other life forms—such as ourselves. But people like Albert Schweitzer stress that we must strive to do the least harm possible to other living beings:

> Whenever I injure life of any kind, I must be quite clear as to whether this is necessary or not. I ought never to pass the limits of the unavoidable, even in apparently insignificant cases. The countryman who has mowed down a thousand blossoms in his meadow as fodder for his cows should take care that on his way home he does not, in wanton pastime, switch off the head of a single flower growing on the edge of the road, for in so doing [he] injures life without being forced to do so by necessity.

## RESPECT: THE ENERGETIC RESONANCE

In an earlier chapter, we discussed how energies permeate the universe. When a person's life becomes grounded in respect, sensitive people can perceive a shift in their energy field. In the same way, some people tend to attract animals to them because animals instinctively sense that they are friendly and kind. The cultivation of respect in our lives—respect toward ourselves, other people, animals, plants, and other living beings—helps create the *total energetic expression* of who we are. Since devas relate at an energetic level rather than on the basis of our outer appearance, the quality and tenor of our energy are vital for any meaningful relationship with them. For example, a callous individual walking into the forest with the sole intent of clear-cutting a stand of trees would inspire fear among the nature spirits, while a person entering the forest with at attitude of respect and gratitude would inspire confidence, even if his journey involved tree cutting.

A person who has not cultivated respect in his life would not only be unreceptive to the benign energies of nature, but would also arouse distrust and fear among the resident nature spirits. A person for whom respect is the keynote of his or her being, however, inspires trust and openness among members of the angelic kingdom. It is almost like the nature beings would say, "This person is a friend." Such persons will be attracted to the members of the angelic hierarchy who will best resonate with their loving, respectful energy. This foundation is essential for the safest, clearest, and most refined level of interspecies communication and communion.

# 6
# Humility

*Humility, that low, sweet root*
*From which all heavenly virtues shoot.*
**—Thomas Moore, The Loves of the Angels**

Humility is our "safety net" when we work with nature spirits. It prevents us from indulging in the very human trait of trying to control nature from a place of ego gratification, or otherwise manipulating nature or other living beings so that they will do our bidding.

Humility is the psychological aspect of grounding. It implies letting go of mental control and relinquishing idealized images of ourselves as human beings. The term "humble" traces its origin to the Latin word *humus,* meaning "the ground." In modern English, humus is a dark brown or black substance resulting from the slow decomposition and oxidation of organic matter that forms the soil in which plants grow.

Being humble does not mean having an inferiority complex. While humility teaches us that we are not the center of the universe, neither are we as mere grains of sand on the beach. "Humility is to make a right estimate of one's self," said Charles H. Spurgeon. "It is no humility for a man to think less of himself than he ought, though it might rather puzzle him to do that."

Humility helps us gain a balanced perception of ourselves in relation to the rest of the living world. Discovering the quality of humility not only permits us to be open to new ideas and to other people's points of view, but makes us more receptive to nature and to the information and inspiration the devas have to share with us.

# A SELF-CENTERED TRADITION

We humans are, by nature, a self-centered race of beings. Our self-centeredness has played a fundamental role in our survival as a species. Our early ancestors needed a strong sense of self to protect themselves and their families in an often hostile environment. They needed to be concerned about themselves as individuals in order to develop strategies to defend themselves from harm and ensure an adequate food supply for members of their immediate group.

Self-centeredness is necessary for learning and growth, for developing our innate talents such as learning how to hunt or play a musical instrument. It is an aspect of our being that makes us distinct from other beings; it is a part of our character that helps us become the unique individuals that we are. Having a strong sense of self is not inherently evil or wrong. It is a necessary part of our evolutionary journey to experience individualization and to see life from a self-centered viewpoint rather than from a more universal and selfless point of view.

Ideally, we can retain these qualities of self-identity and individualization while discovering a broader sense of identity with all the rest of creation. For example, Australian aboriginals recognize individuality—they value each person's artistic ability, hunting prowess, or musical talent—but this is accompanied by an understanding that the individual is also part of a larger community with a highly complex kinship system. In addition to a healthy balance between self-centeredness and community-centeredness, tribal members often have a broad definition of community that includes other animals, as well as trees, rivers, winds, and rocks. Like other indigenous peoples, the Aborigines view this larger community as a type of extended family. Their perspective is based on the understanding that we are dependent on other forms of life for our survival, learning, and enjoyment. The famous prayer of St. Francis beautifully expresses this expanded view of nature:

> Praised be you, my Lord, for Brother Wind,
> And for the air—cloudy and serene—and every kind of weather,
> By which you give sustenance to your creatures.
> Praised be you, my Lord, for Brother Fire,
> By whom you light the night,
> And he is beautiful and jocund and robust and strong.
> Praised be you, my Lord, for our sister Mother Earth,

*Who sustains and governs us,*
*And produces various fruits with colored flowers and herbs. . . .*

As humanity began to lose the primal foundation of connectedness to the natural world, our equilibrium between selfhood and community became distorted. Individualism and self-centeredness intensified to the point of exaggeration. As our ancestors moved to cities and towns, their social interaction placed less emphasis on cooperation and inclusiveness and more on personal needs and the needs of the immediate family unit. Racial identity, religious identity, financial status, material wealth, and political influence were the preoccupations of early civilizations in Mesopotamia, Greece, and Rome. The natural world began to be viewed as a source of wealth, power, and status rather than as the Mother and sustainer of humankind. Beginning in ancient times, the great forests of Europe and the Middle East were systematically destroyed in order to build temples, forts, houses, and ships. Enormous quantities of wood were used to fuel smelters for manufacturing items of bronze, copper, and other metals. Competitiveness, greed, envy, and comparison emerged as characteristics that continue to be reflected in societies throughout the world today, especially in large cities.

As we moved farther and farther away from the natural world, the human perspective on life continued to shift from an intuitive and feeling level toward a more mental and analytical one. We no longer saw ourselves as a tiny part of the natural scheme of things. Our image of ourselves as human beings took on a greater degree of self-importance, a view reflected in religious and philosophical teachings. The rise of Christianity signaled a growing split between nature and spirit, "making the distinction between the natural and the supernatural so strict as to come near to depriving nature of the inner spirit that breathes through all things," writes the Islamic scholar Seyyed Hossein Nasr.

The Bible teaches that humans as a group are superior to the rest of creation, and that humankind is to have "dominion" over cattle, fish, birds, and "over all the earth, and over every creeping thing that creepeth upon the earth" (Gen. 1:26). Humans are the self-appointed "kings of the mountain," entitled to do with our estranged "relatives" as we wish.

The modern-day results of this age-old human arrogance are pollution, the destruction of the ozone layer, and the greenhouse effect. Changes in climate due to deforestation, increased incidence of immune-deficiency diseases among humans, and increasing crop failures due to a disappear-

*Osorno Volcano and Petrohué Waterfall, near Puerto Montt, Chile*

ing ozone layer warn that the health of our planetary home is severely compromised. We are destroying the Earth Mother who has provided us a home and who nourishes us throughout our lifetime.

Indigenous peoples, like the Shuar, Navajo, and Maori have always been humble enough to realize that humans cannot live without nature, but nature can live without us. Life on Earth is likely to continue in some form or another with or without us humans, just as it continued after the extinction of the dinosaurs millions of years ago. Many forms of life will not be (or have not been) able to survive the continued ravages of pollution and deforestation. Other species—consider the incredible evolutionary longevity of cockroaches, alligators, and ginkgo trees, for example—will continue to adapt and thrive in a changing world environment. If humans as a species hope to survive, a fundamental change in our relationship with nature is essential.

## HUMILITY: THE GREAT LEVELER

Humility can help us to change our "dysfunctional" relationship with the natural world. Humility involves surrendering our cherished perspectives to new possibilities. It requires us to let go of mental control and give over to our heart-centered feelings, to our best natural instincts, and to an unvarnished awareness of reality. Humility also calls upon us to give voice to our doubts and confusion, open to the possibility that what we have been taught in the past may indeed no longer be true.

Several years ago, I visited a close friend in Brazil who was recovering from pancreatic cancer. When he first learned that his condition was terminal, he refused medical attention. Only six months later, however, medical examinations revealed that the cancer had completely disappeared. He has now been cancer-free for over six years.

My friend told me that his healing began through ingesting a drink known in Portuguese as *daime*. Also called ayahuasca and *yaje*, it is used primarily by members of native cultures throughout the Amazon, including the Miraña, the Shuar, and the Machiguenga under the guidance of tribal shamans. In Brazil, daime is made of two sacred plants of the rainforest, the *cipó jagube* vine *(Banisteriopsis caapi)* and leaves of the *folha chacrona (Psychotria viridis)*, a small tree of the coffee family.

My friend told me that in addition to its healing properties, daime also brings about an altered state of consciousness, like peyote or certain kinds of "magic" mushrooms. My friend belongs to an ecospiritual group that uses daime to achieve spiritual unfoldment and to learn how to live more in harmony with the natural world; he invited me to participate in a religious ceremony that was to take place later that week.

Despite my inherent skepticism and visions of cultists drinking poisoned Kool-Aid at the ill-fated Jonestown community in Guyana, I decided to accept his invitation. I knew that few people survive pancreatic cancer, even when they undergo chemotherapy, radiation, or surgery. I figured that if daime could enable my friend to be healed of a terminal disease, it wouldn't do me any harm.

The ceremony was held in a simple church built in a clearing within the forest. More than one hundred people were present, including several who had journeyed from Rio de Janeiro and São Paulo especially for the event. After drinking a glass of daime, church members assembled in rows for the ceremony, which involved singing hymns and dancing in formation. The ceremony began at sundown, and would continue until the Sun rose the following morning.

Several minutes after ingesting the bitter coffee-colored liquid, I began to experience a rather pleasant sensation of greater sensitivity to both my body and the people around me. But a few minutes later, fear, and then terror, began to take over: I began to feel pressure in my chest, dizziness, and a heaviness in my arms and legs. I also became nauseated and had to run outside the church and vomit. I felt totally out of control of my mind and bodily functions. My discomfort and fear led me to believe that I was going to die. I had never experienced anything like that before.

At that pivotal moment, I remember falling to my knees and tearfully asking God to spare my life. I asked forgiveness for my arrogance, pride, and hurtful actions in the past. I asked that my life not be taken from me, and affirmed that I would do whatever was necessary to change. I had never prayed with such intensity before, and I imagined that I made quite a spectacle of myself in front of the other participants in the ceremony, who were singing hymns and moving with the music.

Suddenly I felt the presence of a type of angelic—devic—being or guide, whom I identified as being one of the angels mentioned in the Cabala. I perceived him to be both exceedingly kind and very serious. He informed me that I was not going to die that evening, and that the pain, nausea, and fear were there to allow me to feel more compassion for people who were truly ill as opposed to hypochondriacs like myself who often imagined themselves to be sick. I was also told that the intense physical discomfort would make me humble and allow me to be open to

84

the teachings that the daime had to offer me. Although my physical discomfort did not completely disappear until the end of the ceremony, I became more receptive to a "course of instruction" in the subtle realms that lasted until dawn.

## LEARNING HUMILITY FROM NATURE

Nature herself is often the greatest teacher of humility. Earth changes such as earthquakes, volcanic eruptions, hurricanes and cyclones, tornadoes, floods and forest fires often leave lasting impressions on those of us who have witnessed such events. "Natural disasters" leave us with a realization of what is truly important in life and an abiding respect for the powers of nature.

I remember watching a news report on television after a powerful earthquake destroyed parts of Mexico City several years ago. One tearful survivor stood outside what remained of a luxurious apartment building expressing his thanks to God that his wife and children were spared. Although he lost all of his material possessions, he realized that his family was far more important to him than his apartment, furniture, or automobile. The report went on to show a number of famous actors and singers (who would probably never perform manual labor under normal circumstances) digging through the rubble for survivors, serving coffee, and tending to the wounded. Their lack of self-centeredness and self-importance reflected the essence of true humility.

Few of us look forward to being involved in an earthquake or hurricane. Yet by consciously striving to become more aware of the powers of nature during such events, we can more thoroughly integrate the concept of humility into the depths of our being.

A far more pleasurable way to learn humility from nature is to enjoy the majesty of nature's most impressive masterpieces. Visiting large waterfalls, canyons, mountains, lakes, and trees—especially planetary power spots like the Grand Canyon, Ayers Rock, Stonehenge, Mount Fuji, or Victoria Falls—can transform one's entire outlook on life.

## DISCOVERING OUR MISCONCEPTONS

An important aspect of inner discovery involves being on the lookout for self-deception. Unresolved feelings of guilt may lead us to belittle our positive qualities, talents, and capacities, which can prevent us from using our mistakes as stepping-stones to new understanding. Guilt may also make us feel undeserving of communion with nature and other good things of life because we do not live up to the idealized images of who we would like to become. But just because we have made mistakes in the past does not mean that we are untrustworthy or undeserving. As human beings, we are *evolving* toward a higher level of consciousness. Making mistakes and becoming aware of our shortcomings are part of this process.

"Humility," Dag Hammarskjold once said, "is just as much the opposite of self-abasement as it is of self-exultation."

> To be humble is *not to make comparisons*. Secure in its reality, the self is neither better nor worse, bigger nor smaller, than anything else in the universe. It *is*—is nothing, yet at the same time is one with everything.

Paradoxically, some people who have embraced humility feel that they are special or superior to those who have not discovered it. For some of us, there is also a temptation to feel special because we commune with nature spirits. Like other acts of pride and specialness, they often stem from being disconnected from nature in the first place. They lead to feelings of insecurity and the need for compensation from the outside. Remember that many who have felt deeply connected to the Earth (especially shamans, medicine people, gardeners, and farmers) do not feel special or egotistical about their connection. They are who they are, and they work with humility and diligence to serve the human, animal, plant, mineral, and devic communities around them.

## ASKING THE TREES FOR HELP

Humans and trees naturally enjoy a very close relationship, and trees can assist us in experiencing true humility. Not only do trees produce the oxygen that we require for our survival, but they provide us with food, shelter, medicines, protection, and inspiration. Like trees, humans live in the vertical dimension. Because the tree remains in one place throughout its life and a human moves constantly about, we complement each other perfectly. The tree can share information gained from the stability of

*Cypress, near Pont Lobos, California*

being grounded in the Earth and living in one place all its life, while we can energetically share our experience as a being on the move.

With reverence and respect, approach a tree you feel especially friendly toward. Take hold of it and ask sincerely—not from your head, but from your heart—for help to become humble, to become aware of your primal connection with the Earth Mother, and to see your life in true perspective. Pray to give over to the power of healing, regeneration, and wisdom that is available to you. Know that such a connection and a communion is indeed your birthright as a son or daughter of the Earth Mother. Be receptive to what the tree has to offer: the abundance, the wisdom, the power, the life that it has to share.

As you strive to renew and deepen such contacts, the blocks to humility will gradually be removed. The power of wisdom will remove them. For wisdom—true wisdom—is a destroyer of arrogance, of separateness, and of disrespect. It leads each of us, through self-awareness, honesty, and truth, to the hidden treasure of humility—our connection to all of life and to the beings who look forward to renewing our lost relationship once again.

# HUMILITY, HUMOR, AND POWER

A sense of humor is essential when we embark on any spiritual discipline, and it can be an important quality when we are exploring unresolved aspects of our relationship with nature. Many Native American tribes believed that too much seriousness and too much power could lead to imbalance, which could adversely affect both the welfare of the community and the surrounding natural environment. Sacred fools and clowns often participated in even the most important tribal rites, and a vast number of lighthearted activities—including gambling and hoop and pole games—were essential aspects of Native American community life. Among the Inuit, song festivals are ritually structured and planned, yet they often include spontaneous expressions of drama, joking, and satire. According to one Inuit proverb, "Those who know how to play can easily leap over the adversities of life. And one who knows how to sing and laugh never brews mischief."

Nature spirits work for the glory of the Earth Mother, and they exist to do her will through the guidance, manifestation, and evolution of form. The primary component of any request we may have when working with nature spirits must be—in the true spirit of humility—to do the will of the

Earth Mother. If not, we are crossing the line into the realms of Black Magic by manipulating the forces of nature for our own selfish ends.

In surrendering our will to that of the Earth Mother, we do not become weak, but powerful. We ally ourselves with the forces of evolution and love. Learning how to respond to these deeper instincts is truly an act of strength.

Discovering humility and practicing it daily may not always be easy. It requires ongoing attention and honesty with ourselves. Confrontation of illusion, questioning our motives and intentions, striving to keep things simple, accepting our imperfections, maintaining a sense of humor, and living in day-to-day reality are the small yet important personal steps needed to cultivate natural humility in all of our endeavors.

A final component of humility is realizing that our learning, development, health, and experience must exist in the overall context of helping and serving others. We realize that each of us is a cell in both the body of humanity, as well as that of the Earth Mother. This realization enables us to receive with one hand and share with the other. We do not keep what we have been given strictly for our personal benefit alone.

Through sharing our victories as well as our struggles, we empower others around us and aid in the process of evolution of all living beings. This recognition is not only an act of true humility, it is a recognition of the reality of our life's journey on Earth.

# DISCOVERY

# 7

# Preparation

When we plan a trip to another city or country, careful preparation is often necessary. In the days preceding a journey, we usually make a list of the items we will need for the trip, such as clothing, shoes, toiletries, guidebooks, passport, and currency. Special attention is often given to what we may need for that "big night out," as well as to what may be required in case of an emergency. The more careful travelers among us also investigate the proposed route of the journey and make sure that we have the needed addresses and the instructions on how to arrive at our specific destination. Finally, if the main purpose of the trip is to visit a friend or relative, we may want to bring along an appropriate gift for our host or hostess. As with any important journey, careful planning is needed when we are going to visit with nature spirits. Travelers may have three major questions regarding such a journey: Where to go? What to wear? and What to bring?

## WHERE TO GO?

We mentioned earlier that different individuals resonate best with specific places in nature. One person may be drawn to a beach setting, while another will be attracted to the mountains or the forest. According to the

Candomblé tradition of Africa and Brazil, each person has two primary areas of attraction that are the most appropriate for contacting those nature spirits most compatible with his or her soul essence. For example, I feel a strong resonance with mountains and windy places; all mountains and all windy places would be the best destinations if I wanted to communicate with nature spirits or devas.

As a rule, the largest and most magnificent natural forms contain the most powerful devic energy. A place like Niagara Falls would have far more devic energy than that of a three-foot-high waterfall in a city park. It is always worthwhile to visit "planetary power spots" like the Grand Canyon, Crater Lake, or Mount Fuji, but most of us can do important work in the many smaller, less well-known places that are easily within our reach—for instance, in the local park, or even in our own backyard.

While it may be true that we can visit any beach, any mountain, or any river for devic communication and communion, many of us feel an attraction to a specific place in nature that may, in fact, be completely overlooked by others. This may be a particular tree that we have long been attracted to, or a place along a stream that has always brought us a feeling of peace and integration. If such is the case with you, then go to this spot. In addition to being a place you enjoy being in, you probably have already established a subconscious relationship with the angelic being or beings who make their home at or near that special place.

Before you decide to go to a particular spot, it is always a good idea to meditate on what you need. Why do you wish to commune with a nature being today? What do you hope to accomplish? Do you feel like going a long distance, or do you want to be close to home? What type of energy are you yearning to connect with? What kind of place (or places) are you especially attracted to? By asking such questions before you undertake your journey, you become more aware of your deeper needs and will be more sensitized to a particular energy in nature that will help you the most.

Although nature spirits exist throughout the natural world, they are most often found at obvious physical forms such as waterfalls, cliffs, mountaintops, volcanoes, forests, and lakes. A large natural form like a lake or a mountain will probably be the home of a vast multitude of nature spirits. They will likely be of different sizes, will generate different energies, and perform many different tasks. If you visit a mountaintop, for example, you will not only find mountain devas, but may also perceive the presence of wind devas, tree devas, flower devas, and devas connected to outcroppings of rock. Some devas tend to shy away from

94

*Costa Rica River, near Guápiles, Costa Rica*

humans, but others are definitely more "friendly," especially when approached with a sense of appreciation and respect. By being both sensitive to our surroundings and clear in our intent, we will more easily attract the type of devic energy we need.

Some places in nature contain higher concentrations of devic energy because of their size, location, or combinations of different natural elements. By becoming more aware of these locations, and perceptive of the energy they generate, you will be able to access a more powerful devic presence.

## Rivers and Streams

Flowing water is often a powerful place for healing, cleansing, and for resolving inner conflicts. This is one reason why white-water rafters or inner-tube enthusiasts feel so invigorated and refreshed after a journey down a river or stream. Rivers have been considered sacred by many of the world's peoples and are the abode of powerful spirit beings. In ancient China, He Bo (Bing-yi) was the divine ruler of all rivers. Until the end of the Zhou dynasty (256 B.C.) a maiden was sacrificed to him every year. Among the Aztecs, Chalchihuitlicue was the goddess of flowing waters, and the spouse of Tlaloc, the powerful rain god. In the Candomblé tradition, flowing fresh waters are in the domain of Oshoun, who is connected with romantic love, marriage, and human fertility. Oshoun is also the goddess of prosperity, believed to bring prosperity to those who honor her.

Special "power spots" along a river or stream include places where rapids or waterfalls exist. Electric companies often build generators in these places of high water flow, because more energy can be produced there. By the same token, the amount of "subtle" energy generated is greater in these places as well. Power spots may be found where a tributary joins with the primary stream or where a major change in the depth of the water changes the rate of water flow. Other places of more intense energy are found where there is a strong change of direction of the water flow or at any spot along a river or stream that is near an important natural form such as a large tree, boulder, or cliff. Islands located in the middle of a river are often places of more intense energy, so they are good locations for healing and other creative work.

## Lakes

A lake is an excellent destination for those seeking quiet meditation or contemplation. It is a place for centering our energies and focusing on the depths of our inner being. Lakes were held in world mythology to be sources of both natural forms and creative energy, and were often the homes of powerful gods and goddesses. Among the Inca and Aymara, Lake Titicaca was the abode of Viracocha, the creator of mountains, plains, and people. In what is now Mexico, the early Aztecs worshiped Lake Texcoco, which was known as Tonanhueyatl, or "our mother great water." Because lakes were closely linked to agricultural and human fertility, pilgrimages were often made to the shores of Texcoco and other lakes, where people would offer green stones, jewelry, and even living sacrifices. In the Candomblé tradition, lakes (as well as marshes and swamps) are connected with the deva Nanan, the "grandmother" of the Brazilian orishas who is respected for her age and wisdom.

Lakes are vital for the spiritual and physical health of the planet. After meditating by the shores of beautiful Lake Nahuel Huapí near Bariloche, Argentina, I recorded the following message in my notebook:

> It is vitally important that the waters of the Earth Mother are kept unsullied, for they are essential to all life. And not just to your life, but

*Lake Nahuel Huapí, near Bariloche, Argentina*

to all life in all gradients of existence. A clean body of water such as myself is as essential to the health of the Earth Mother as a clean glass of water is to yours.

Let the truth of stewardship of the Earth wash over you like my waves on this shore. Gradually let the need of protecting the Earth wash over you and become an integral part of your being. Open yourself up to nature, and little by little, a deep commitment will be made. Learn more about the mysteries of nature. Learn how to protect nature. And plant the seeds of wisdom and compassion wherever you go.

Know that the Earth will not be saved by a select few. She will be saved by a *select many*. She will be saved by those of you who accept the dual mantle of Earth stewardship and spiritual leadership. The Earth will not be saved by the prisoners. She will be saved by those who are free, by those who are responsive, by those who are committed, by those who are unafraid.

There are many individual power spots in and around lakes. As with a stream or river, any place where there is an exceptional change of depth (such as a shelf), or the deepest part of the lake itself, can be a place of enhanced energy. A location on the lake above an underground spring that feeds the lake is always an important power spot, which can often be accessed for healing and revitalization. Almost any point along the lakeshore (where the land meets the water) is a good location for stronger energy, but "promontory points," where the land juts out into the lake, are especially important. Islands have long been considered sacred by native cultures, in part because they were considered the homes of angelic beings. Two islands in Lake Titicaca, for example, were dedicated to the sun father (Inti) and the moon mother (Mama Ouilla) by the Inca and the Aymará.

## Mountains and Valleys

Mountains are among the most sacred places on Earth, and many native traditions speak of powerful gods inhabiting their peaks. In Tibet, the female mountain deity is known as the Great Goddess of Buddhism, Dolma Tara. Mount Kailas (also known as Kang Rinpoche, the Precious Snow Jewel) is so spiritually powerful that it is considered by the Tibetans to be the *axis mundi*, or the center of the world. Among the Navajo, mountains are also power centers imbued with intelligence and vital force. According to Peter Gold in *Navajo and Tibetan Sacred Wisdom*, one model of the Navajo geomantic universe includes four outer sacred mountains, what we know as Mount Taylor, Blanca Peak, San Francisco Peak, and Hesperus Peak. In Candomblé, mountains are said to be ruled by Oshala, the father of the devas and the grandfather of all mortals. Mountain devas are among the most powerful members of the angelic hierarchy.

Oshala and his assisting devas can be found throughout mountains and valleys, the highest concentrations residing at both the depths and the heights. For example, the lowest floor of Death Valley in California would be the home of powerful devic beings, as would be the summit of Mount Logan in Canada or Mount Kosciuzco in Australia. Mountains of volcanic origin are especially potent locations of devic power, especially at the base of the crater within the volcano itself. This is not to say that there are no devic presences along the outside slopes as well, with greater power toward the summit. Active volcanoes—with their tremendous geothermal activity—are homes of extremely powerful devic beings, but contact with them is best experienced from a distance!

In a mountain or valley setting, devas are most likely to be found at any unusual crevice, rock formation, large outcropping of rocks, ravine, depression, or elevation that tends to differ from the surrounding terrain.

*Puntiagudo Volcano and Lake Todos Los Santos, Chile*

This is especially true when you find a dramatic change of topography, such as a cliff or a ravine. Two outstanding examples of such places are the White Cliffs of Dover and the Copper Canyon in Mexico.

## Forests and Trees

In Brazil, forests and jungles are the domain of Oshossi, a restless devic being connected with forest animals and the healing powers of medicinal plants. The forests are special places for communicating with nature spirits, especially those involved with the evolution of trees. When you visit a forest or park, be especially aware of any tree that appears "different": one of an unusual shape for its species, a tree of an advanced age, or a tree of very large size. Trees found at the summit of a mountain or on a promontory point, such as a spit of land overlooking an ocean or lake, can also be a place of strong devic energy. Such a tree will tend to visibly or energetically stand out from other trees in the immediate area. An unusually dense community of older trees, or a grove of three or more trees planted in a circle, triangle, or square are also special places of heightened devic energy. In Prospect Park in Brooklyn, there is a unique grove of nine elm trees planted in a circle. Now more than fifty years old, this circle of trees is a magnet to people seeking peace, relaxation, and healing in an otherwise difficult urban environment. Much of the inspiration and guidance for this book came from the devic presences who reside in this beautiful grove.

Finally, any tree that is planted near a house of worship, a shrine, or a monument can be a special source of devic power. By the same token, look for any tree that has already been recognized as a sacred tree, a historical tree, a wish tree, a medicine tree, or a tree shrine by the local or indigenous community. The famous Angel Oak near Charleston, South Carolina, the Colonel Armstrong Redwood near Guerneville, California, or the enormous tule tree (Mexican cypress) near Oaxaca, Mexico, are but three outstanding examples of such special trees.

## The Ocean

The ocean can be a powerful source of healing power, inspiration, and devic consciousness. The ocean is, in essence, the original home from which humans have evolved. Many of us are familiar with myths about Poseidon, the ocean god of the Greeks, and Neptune, the ocean god of the Romans. The Chinese considered the sea to be the domain of Yu-ch'iang, who is also a wind god. The Inuit know the sea-goddess as Sedna, whom they both revere and fear; only a shaman is believed to have the power to withstand the sight of her.

In the Candomblé, Umbanda, and Santería traditions, the ocean is the domain of Yemanjá (Yemayá), the deva who represents the maternal forces of nature. She is considered a serene and peaceful nature being, but she is also emotionally unstable, with a strong temper and unforgiving nature. Brazilian fishermen respect Yemanjá and often offer prayers to her before they embark on an ocean voyage.

Most people who work with Yemanjá and her helpers do so from on or near the shore, which affords the greatest degree of safety. Others may work with the ocean devas from boats or through snorkeling or scuba diving. Swimmers should be especially careful when working with Yemanja, because the danger of drowning increases when a swimmer is preoccupied with spiritual matters.

The energy of the ocean is extremely powerful; nearly all locations along the ocean coastline are good places to visit. However, the forces tend to be greater where a cliff, ravine, or escarpment meets the ocean itself, or where a river or stream flows into the ocean. Greater energy can be found at places where the ocean floor undergoes a dramatic change

*Pacific Ocean, San Francisco, California*

of depth, such as a continental shelf, trench, or mountain range, perhaps because of the presence of mountain devas connected with these geological forms. The devic presences associated with these places can affect sensitive travelers who are voyaging by boat or plane above.

## Winds

Windy places are among the most exciting to experience, and are often best visited when we need new ideas, or we want resolve to problems that have not been easy to work through. Varpulis was a powerful wind god among the pre-Christian Slavs, while the Jukun of Nigeria worship a wind god they know as Awo. The early Japanese considered Take-haya-susa-no-wo-no-mikoto the most terrifying of the gods, depicted in myths as being "always in a fury." In Candomblé, it is taught that Yansan is the goddess of the winds; she is connected to Shangó, the deva of thunder and storms (as well as caves, cliffs, and large rocks).

Wind devas are especially present in any location where the winds are unusually active on a permanent, ongoing basis, at places like canyons, waterfalls, mountaintops, or shorelines. They are also associated with high places in general, as mountain climbers and parachutists would attest. If you live in a large city, you can contact wind devas by standing on the observation deck or roof of a tall building. In addition, wind associated with a dramatic change in weather patterns (such as a storm or hurricane) indicates that devic activity ordinarily associated with winds is enhanced. If you can find a sheltered spot during a storm, for example (yet permitting yourself to be close to the elements like wind and rain), you can avail yourself of enhanced access to the devic presences who involve themselves with powerful meteorological activity.

## Fire

A volcanic eruption or forest fire could provide unique (not to mention memorable) opportunities for communion with powerful devas, but be careful that the welfare of your physical well-being is not compromised! Safer places for communion with salamanders (devas related to the element of fire) are volcanoes (preferably semiactive ones that can be approached safely), as well as thermal-related phenomena like geysers, fumaroles, and hot mineral springs. The world is generously blessed with these special places, especially in areas of seismic activity. Because they often involve alchemical processes, such places are often connected with favoring transformational events in the human psyche, such as relinquishing old patterns, formulating new ideas, gaining new perspectives, undergoing initiation, and activating the process of healing.

# WHAT TO WEAR?

When I first began to communicate with nature spirits, I had believed that wearing certain colors was necessary in order to do spiritual or healing work with different nature spirits. One day I asked a tree deva which colors would be the most appropriate to wear in its presence. The answer that came back surprised me: "The clothing you should wear is humility and respect." The deva gave me the impression that we humans place too much emphasis on outer appearances, while we often ignore the state of our underlying consciousness. As mentioned earlier, devas tend to respond best to sincere, heartfelt feelings, and they work with us from that inner place of resonance. They are not particularly interested in what we look like or how we are dressed.

Nonetheless, different metaphysical traditions place an emphasis on the color of clothing for certain rituals or religious practices, and while

*Villarrica Volcano, near Pucón, Chile*

our attitude and feelings are of primary importance when communing with nature spirits, appropriately colored clothing (of natural fibers like cotton, silk, or wool) and jewelry can be beneficial adjuncts to this sacred work. Remember that there are no hard and fast rules regarding color; in fact, different cultures and religions (not to mention individuals) assign different meanings to the same color. For example, in the West, black is associated with death, while in China, the color associated with death is white.

*Red* is the most vibrant color of the spectrum and has played an important role in the life of many early cultures. The ancient Greeks wore red robes to symbolize sacrifice and love, while the Hindus associated red with fire. Red gowns were often worn by brides on their wedding day in early China, where the color red symbolized innocence. The Hebrews saw red as symbolic of both sacrifice and sin, while the early Egyptians considered red to be the primary symbol of power. Red is a passionate color; because it can increase our overall energy level and stimulate sexual feelings, it is often associated with love, passion, and romance. Red is physical, masculine, and dynamic. It is a "take charge" color, a "yang" color. It can be worn to stimulate passion, power, and greater energy. The Candomblé tradition of Africa and Brazil teaches that red is the favorite color of the tempestuous deva Yansan, the goddess of winds and lightning.

*Yellow* is a color often associated with the Sun, and is the color of joy, creativity, humor, and conceptual thinking. The early Greeks represented this color as the element of air and viewed it as a symbol of God and creation. In Candomblé, yellow is the color of Oshoun, the goddess associated with romantic love, marriage, and fertility. In occultism, yellow is seen as the color of intellect and the powers of thought. By wearing clothes that are yellow in color, one's mental bodies can be strengthened and developed. Wearing yellow will help create a feeling of joy and stimulate better communication with others.

The color *green* has always been associated with nature, fecundity, and everlasting life. It is the color of expansion, growth, and optimism. In early Christian times, green symbolized immortality and was often found on the robes of saints. Because this color is so closely associated with the Earth, it was seen as the emblem of learning by the Druids and other nature-oriented peoples. In occultism, the color green is closely associated with healing, sympathy, and adaptability. It is probably the best color to wear when you want to heal a relationship or work on physical healing, or when you want to create feelings of harmony, expansion, and abundance. It is also an ideal color to wear when you want to communicate with devas associated with trees and other plants.

*Blue* follows red as our most favored color. Blue symbolizes sensitivity, receptivity, wisdom, detachment, acceptance, and sharing. It often adorned the ceilings of Egyptian temples, and it was seen by the Druids as the color of harmony and truth. To the early Christians, blue was the color of piety, while pale blue symbolized peace and prudence. Occultists have taught that blue is connected to feelings of devotion and religious mysticism. It represents the spiritual and feminine side of our beings, the "yin" side. Wearing blue can stimulate inner peace, compassion, and receptivity. In the Candomblé tradition, when working with the devas of the forest—the realm of Oshossi—light blue is the preferred color, while dark blue is suggested when working with Ogun, the deva connected with outcroppings and veins of iron; Nanan, the goddess of the lakes, is said to resonate well with the energy of people wearing aquamarine blue.

The color *purple* is considered by teachers of metaphysics to be the color of the Age of Aquarius, and it is associated with spiritual devotion mixed with affection. As the combination of the masculine (red) and feminine (blue), this color represents sexual union as well as mystical union. Among early Jews, this color, and its more bluish hue, violet, symbolized splendor and dignity, while early Christians associated purple with suffering and sacrifice. Purple is also connected to Uranus, the planet of spiritual knowledge. Today, hues of purple—including violet and lavender—are considered "spiritual" colors that inspire devotion and spiritual feelings.

*White* is the union of all colors, and it has always been associated with purity. It is said that white was the color of the Egyptian Horus, who was born of both the masculine and feminine principles of the universe. White was considered the color of joy by early Jews and Persians alike, and it always has been the symbol of chastity, innocence, and purity among Christians. We mentioned earlier that the ancient Chinese saw white as the color of death. White is believed to transcend all other colors. When shining in the human aura, it signifies "true spirit." This is why white (either alone or in combination with other colors) is recommended when we work with nature spirits or devas. In fact, when working with the deva Oshala (the orisha of the mountains) or with Yemanjá (the goddess of the oceans), Candomblé priests and priestesses recommend the exclusive use of white.

Gold, orange, brown, and gray are formed by mixing some of the primary colors mentioned above, and they often share a number of symbolic meanings with these colors. Depending on the combination, they can increase or decrease the intensity of a primary color. The color orange, for example, is believed to intensify the mental properties of yellow, while it both reduces and intellectualizes the raw power of red. It is closely associated with courage, illumination, harvest, and manifestation.

*Black,* a "color" that is actually the absence of both color and light, is closely associated with death, destruction, protection, and mystery. The early Christians saw black as a symbol of both death and regeneration, while the Native Americans considered black to represent the lower worlds. Astrologers believe that black is connected to the planet Saturn and the zodiacal sign of Capricorn, both symbolic of initiation and self-realization. Black clothing can be very intense and has the tendency to accentuate our lower or shadow nature. As we will discuss in a later chapter, the resonance produced by the unrecognized and unresolved shadow self may cause difficulties in our work with residents of the subtler realms. For this reason, black clothing is generally *not* recommended when we seek to commune with nature spirits.

Some of us are very aware of our personal colors. Although I tend to wear a variety of colors on a daily basis, I find that navy blue and white are "my" colors when I do any type of serious spiritual work. Whatever your own colors may be, white is always a good color as part of our overall outfit when we wish to work with devic beings.

An awareness of the colors we wear is an added means of self-expression and communication with devas and the universal energies of which we are a part. For this reason, the colors we wear should always be chosen carefully, especially when we wish to work with the subtle aspects of nature.

## WHAT TO BRING?

Some people feel comfortable wearing jewelry or carrying crystals when they visit with nature spirits. Crystals are not dead matter, but very dense living forms that exist at a specific rate of vibration. Among Native American medicine people, *quartz crystals* are often carried in medicine bags or worn as jewelry because they impart certain beneficial energies. Michael Harner in *The Way of the Shaman* explains that a quartz crystal is considered the strongest power object among shamans from Latin America to Australia, primarily because of its reputation as a spirit helper whose material and spiritual natures are the same. Among the Wirajeri of Australia, quartz crystals are believed to enable the shaman to achieve heightened states of clairvoyant awareness. As sacred objects, crystals deserve our care and respect.

Crystals can be carried by hand or worn as rings, pendants, or earrings, and when used as part of any sacred ritual, it is always a good idea to cleanse your crystal of energies that were involved in its mining, preparation, transportation, and sale. The easiest way to do this is to soak the crystal in saltwater and leave it in the sunlight for seven days. After rinsing the crystal with fresh water, you may wish to say a prayer over it or make an affirmation of how you would like it to be used: "I pray that this crystal will help keep me grounded and of pure intent." This act of "programming" the crystal is believed to help make it more powerful.

Clear quartz is said to help us connect with higher and/or deeper levels of consciousness, while amethyst (purple quartz) is reputed to calm the mind to help transform and transmute energy. Citrine (orange quartz) is often used to assist our intuitive nature and to help protect us from negative psychic energies. Rose quartz is used to help open up the heart and to calm the emotions, while smokey quartz is good for grounding and mental clarity. Very often people use these stones in combination with each other. The study of crystals (and how to work with them) is fascinating, and many fine books are available for the interested person who wishes to learn more about their mystery.

If you wish to bring religious items—such as crosses, religious images, and other sacred possessions—you should. They are designed to help elevate consciousness and enable us to refine our energies. They also may offer a sense of protection and groundedness.

Material offerings to devas are not required. As subtle beings, devas focus more on the energy that we bring to them rather than a concrete offering alone. Respect, love, wonder, and appreciation are considered the best gifts that a human can bring to a deva, and are very much appreciated by them. But any physical offering, when given from the heart, is also appreciated. (Offerings are discussed in more detail in the next chapter.)

When working with a nature spirit in a remote area, it is always good to bring along practical items like a first-aid kit, flashlight, compass, insect repellent, sunscreen, and pocket knife. Bring adequate food and water if you plan to be out more than several hours. As a writer, I always take along some pens and a notebook when I go to commune with devas, as I often receive guidance and inspiration through writing. Others may want to carry a book of sacred writings, such as a Bible or a prayer book. An artist may bring along a sketch pad and pencils, paints, or chalk, while a person interested in music may want to take a musical instrument when going to visit the devas.

Above all, bring with you a sense of openness and wonder on your journey, and strive to be open to any eventuality. The experience of communing with members of the angelic kingdom is both an adventure and a privilege. For many people, it can be among the most intimate and rewarding experiences they will ever know.

# 8

# Invocation

*The ideal of brotherhood is to draw angels and men, two branches of
the infinite family of God, into close cooperation.*
**—Geoffrey Hodson, The Brotherhood of Angels and of Men**

We mentioned earlier that entering the devas' domain is not unlike
visiting a foreign country for the first time. Although we may have visited
the same physical forest, grove of trees, or waterfall many times before,
we are now doing so with a heightened sense of the deeper, more subtle
realities that reside in that particular spot. A sense of newness and
excitement results from the change in our perspective. In this chapter, we
will explore some of the tools that can help invoke the energies of the
nature spirits and develop a sense of openness within ourselves to allow
us to be more receptive to them.

## CLEANSING AND ALIGNMENT

Before you leave home to visit the domain of the nature beings, take a
shower to cleanse both your physical body and your energy field. While
you shower, visualize your entire being washed clean by the flowing
water. You may also wish to "smudge" yourself, cleansing your energy
field by immersing yourself in sacred smoke (a ritual long practiced by
groups as different as the Roman Catholic Church and many Native
American communities). Sage (available at grocery stores and New Age
shops), alone or in combination with sweetgrass, pine needles, or cedar

chips, is most often used for smudging. Place some sage in a bowl and light it, soon adding small amounts of the other ingredients of your choice. You may also say a prayer over the sage as you light it. When the smoke begins to rise, bring it to your head, face, arms, chest, back, legs, and feet, using your hands or a feather to direct the smoke. If you are with a partner, he or she can smudge you in this manner.

You could also use a commercially made incense for smudging. Each type of incense enhances certain spiritual qualities, so choose your incense based on what kind of work you wish to do with the devas.

*Sandalwood* stimulates the intuition and awakens the desire to merge with higher realms of existence.

*Frankincense* inspires spiritual recognition and helps elevate the mind and emotions.

*Musk* stimulates primal instincts and enables us to come into closer contact with our natural selves.

*Patchouli* awakens the desire for transformation.

*Lotus* inspires the desire to meditate and develops trust and receptivity.

*Lavender* stimulates the yin and yang balance and helps calm the emotions.

Although easily available, commercially prepared incense has usually been handled by many people involved in its collection, manufacture, packaging, transportation, and sale. Often these people leave traces of their energy on the incense according to how they were feeling and what they were thinking at the time they handled it. For this reason, it is a good idea to "demagnetize" the incense before you use it for a sacred purpose like facilitating meditation or cleansing your energy field.

One simple and effective way to demagnetize a stick of incense is to make a circle by joining your thumb and index finger. This creates a concentrated energy field within the circle. Slowly move the stick of incense through the circle with your other hand. By doing so, you "imprint" your energy onto the incense stick. You can also say a prayer over the incense as you light it.

Before venturing out to commune with nature spirits, you may also want to light a new white candle to burn at home during your absence. As you light the candle, make a prayer to the Creator and your spirit guides for protection and support. Be sure to leave the candle burning in a safe place while you are away so that you will have a home to return to!

# MEDITATION

Before entering the realm of the nature spirits, a period of alignment is often recommended. This is best done before you leave home; it can be done again after you enter the devas' sacred space. This can often take the form of meditation or prayer in which we strive to align our thoughts and emotions with our deepest essence or "core." The following method is but one of many ways to do this and can easily be modified according to your personal needs and goals.

1. Find a comfortable place where you can be quiet and alone.
2. Select a comfortable position: perhaps sitting, in a chair or in a cross-legged position on a cushion or rug. If you are outdoors, you may wish to lean against a tree or lie down on the ground.
3. If you prefer to meditate with your eyes open, select something simple to focus your eyes upon, like a candle, a flower, a religious symbol, or some other beautiful object. This will keep your mind from wandering. If you keep your eyes closed, try to visualize a field of white light.
4. Begin to breathe slowly and deeply, becoming aware of your breath as it enters and leaves your body. Each time your mind wanders to other thoughts or is disturbed by outside noises, gently bring your attention back to the easy, natural rhythm of your breathing. If you have trouble keeping your mind on your breath, count each inhalation and exhalation up to ten, and then start over again.
5. As you relax physically, various feelings may come and go. These feelings shouldn't be repressed, but the very act of calmly observing them may cause them to gradually lose their intensity.
6. Gradually intuit and then visualize the concept of oneness with all beings. Express your desire to experience the reality of oneness as an integral part of your life today, either in silence or out loud: "I pray to realize my oneness with nature today." Repeat this visualization slowly several times. You can also express other desires or yearnings you have that you want to integrate into your life during the day. This process is akin to "sending a letter of intent to the universe."

7. After having expressed your keynote visualization, relax and be receptive once more. Continue your relaxed, deep breathing for at least three minutes and feel the sense of oneness living inside your body, near the heart. Feel it streaming out into the room, into the neighborhood, and farther out into the world. End your meditation gradually and in silence.

## ENTERING THE REALM

You are now near the place in nature you have wanted to visit. Take a few moments to ground yourself. Be especially aware of any personal needs in your life at this time. State these needs mentally or express them in words. This will immediately create a resonance to which one or more devas can respond, and it will lead you toward the nature being who will be the most appropriate for you at this time.

With this in mind, approach the devas' realm with a sense of respect. It should feel as though you are entering someone's home for the first time, because you *are* entering someone's home. Most people will come to the devas' realm in respectful silence, while others may hum, sing, or whistle softly while they walk. In general, devas enjoy music, but they tend to dislike loud sounds like shouting, discordant music, and noises made by guns, dirt bikes, and machinery. Maintaining respectful silence is usually best, especially on your first visit.

As you approach the realm of a nature spirit, you may feel its energy from several or more yards away. Ask permission before entering the deva's energy field. If you do not feel welcome there, it is better to go somewhere else. (This should not be taken personally. The deva probably has other work to do and may not be interested in meeting with a human at this time.) However, when you perceive that you are welcome (and this will usually be the case if you've done the preparatory work described earlier), feel gratitude for being where you are at that moment.

As you move into the devas' realm, open yourself to the possibility of whatever may occur. Some of us may have preconceived mental images of what we would like to happen, or what we think will happen, or what we have time for when we are about to work with nature beings; in other words, we want to have mental control over our experience. If you are aware that this current exists in you, work to align and ground yourself once again, and declare something like, "I pray to receive what I need at this time," or (addressing the devas) "I pray to give you my best."

# OFFERINGS

An offering may be given either before or after the act of communion with the deva takes place. We mentioned in the last chapter that offerings are not a *requirement* in order to work with nature beings, because the energy we bring is what they best respond to. But many native peoples have long used sacred tobacco, for example, as an offering in religious ceremonies (and as gifts in general); this is an expression, both physical and spiritual, of honor, respect, and gratitude. The best tobacco to use would contain a minimum of chemical additives. Additive-free tobaccos can be found in Native American supply houses and some New Age stores and bookshops. You may wish to respectfully scatter the tobacco throughout the area or carefully sprinkle it into a stream or around a tree. If you are in a windy place, simply open your hand and let the winds carry it off!

Cut flowers or small personal items such as coins, jewelry, metal objects, crystals, food, or pieces of colored cloth are always appreciated by nature spirits when offered with sincerity. Certain religious traditions like Candomblé or Santería call for very specific types of offerings prepared in special ways. This may involve using candles of a certain color or presenting particular types of food in bowls of a prescribed color or on pieces of cloth or mats of a color most favored by the specific nature being.

For example, a traditional Candomblé offering to Yemanjá, the orisha of the ocean, includes white flowers (especially roses), white candles, and women's perfume. One method calls for going to the beach and digging a hole in the sand in which you will place offerings of candles and flowers. You can also make your offering by simply walking into the ocean carrying a bouquet of white flowers. Begin making your prayer request to Yemanjá as soon as you enter the water, and count the number of waves that wash by. After you meet the seventh wave, cast your flowers (either all together or one by one) into the surf to be received by Yemanjá.

Those who wish to commune with Oshossi, the orisha of wooded areas, forests, and orchards, can place offerings of sliced coconut and green and red fruits like apples, pears, avocados, and papayas in a white bowl laid on a white or light blue cloth selected especially for this purpose. Cooked red corn (if available) is also suggested, in addition to white and light blue flowers and white or blue candles, to be placed in white or transparent candle holders. The flowers should be placed in a white or transparent vase or may simply be arranged around the bowl of fruit.

*Offering to Oshala, including cooked white corn, white flowers, and white candles placed on a white cloth*

In the ceremony to honor Oshossi, the offering is usually presented before communion with the deva has taken place, while with Yemanjá, the offering can be given during communion with the nature spirit. The decision regarding when to make your own particular offering will depend on your intuition. If you decide to include candles in your offering—which this author does not recommend if there is any possibility of a fire hazard—use extreme caution.

Some places—especially those that have been frequently visited by other human beings—may be littered with cans, papers, food, and other trash. Taking a few minutes to clean up the area, or otherwise working to protect the physical area that lies within the energy field of the nature being that is about to assist us, is a vital expression of our concern and respect. This type of offering may be more important than any other. It is much appreciated by the nature spirits, and it helps establish a bond of caring friendship. When we mobilize an expression of caring and concern, we elevate our level of consciousness. As a result, contact with the devas is facilitated.

# INVOCATIONS

You can invoke a nature spirit in a variety of ways;. however, once you are in the devas' realm, the first thing is to ground yourself. You can either stand up or sit down, getting in touch with the Earth in order to become aligned, aware, and inwardly calm. Some people may close their eyes, do deep breathing, and sit quietly in a meditative posture, open to any communication that may take place. Others may pray, chant, or actively ask for help.

When entering the realm of the devas, get in touch with your feelings. Do not insist on taking a prescribed mental approach in your contact with nature. While writing near a tree at the Lankester Botanic Garden in Costa Rica, I recorded the devas' opinion on this point directly:

> The emotional connection one feels toward nature is extremely important. Emotion is one of the primary components of your makeup as human beings. It serves as both a motivator and a "bridge" that propels you and transports you toward new spheres of understanding, new levels of consciousness, and new levels of existence.
>
> We appeal to you that you do not cut off your emotions when you relate to nature. We do not want you to withdraw from this aspect of

your relationship with us. The emotional connection is vital. Devas and humans are far more deeply related than you think, and this relationship extends back to earliest times. The primal link between you humans and us tree devas is ancient and enduring. It is only now being rediscovered as you begin to see how far you have grown apart from us. So when you feel inclined to commune with a tree, it is not unlike seeing a loved one after a long separation. You feel your yearning and the joy of reestablishing your connection with us once again. So feel this connection. Experience your joy!

Geoffrey Hodson offered one simple invocation for communion with a tree deva, to be uttered with a full realization of its meaning: "Greetings beautiful tree. Our [my] life is one with yours." This type of invocation could presumably be used to invoke any devic contact. Other suitable prayers and greetings include: "I come to you in the spirit of oneness"; "My core of love resonates with your core of love"; or "We are both one with the Great Spirit." You can also pray that what you are about to receive will assist you in the healing process, whether it be your own healing or healing between you and nature.

In his classic work *Brotherhood of Angels and of Men*, Hodson shared a special invocation to use when planting vegetables, flowers, or trees:

> Hail, devas of the earth and sky!
> Come to our aid.
> Give fertility to our fields,
> Give life to our seeds,
> That this earth may be fruitful.
> Hail devas of the earth and sky!
> Come to our aid;
> Share with us the labors of our world
> That the divinity within may be set free.

You can also recite prayers you are familiar with, such as the Lord's Prayer, the Hail Mary, or the Gayatri. Prayers of praise to the Great Spirit or Universal Presence are especially useful in invoking devic energy. Sufi mystics offer an especially beautiful prayer of praise:

> The darkness of the night and the brightness of the day, the beams of the sun and the light of the moon, the murmuring of the waters and the whispering of the leaves, the stars of the sky and the dust of the

earth, the stones of the mountains, the sands of the desert, and the waves of the oceans, the animals of water and land praise Thee.

In Brazil, devotees sing hymns of affirmation to different orishas to invoke intuitive contact with them or their helpers. The following is a special hymn for Oshala, the god of the mountains:

> Oxalá meu pai
> Tem pena de nos tem do . . .
> A volta da terra e grande
> E Teu poder ainda e maior . . .
>
> Oshala my father
> Have pity and compassion for us . . .
> The way around the world is vast
> And your power is vaster still . . .

While you are sitting in meditation, you may want to recite one of the mantras (sacred sounds) of praise—such as "Om," "Om Namah Shivaya," "Baroch Ha Shem," or "Insh'Allah"—found among humanity's major religions. When recited with care and respect, these mantras enable us to attract energies that will resonate with our higher selves. As a result, they can bless us deeply.

The open-ended type of invocations provided here offer a high degree of safety, because they are grounded in love and respect. They are heart- and spirit-centered and do not make specific demands. Once we invoke the appropriate nature being, we will have time to ask specific questions later on.

Since the nature beings exist in a hierarchy, we are most likely to attract an elemental or nature spirit whose energy is consonant with ours. Invoking the full power of a mountain deva, for example, could involve accessing a very high level of energy, which could be too much for us to receive at one time. Like using a surge protector to prevent our computers and appliances from being destroyed by sudden bursts of electricity, working with smaller devas helps ensure that we will not be overwhelmed by contact with the devic realms. Since these lesser nature spirits are directly connected with the larger ones, they "step down" the energy and wisdom of the greater devas, making them easier for us to assimilate.

Some individuals recite specific mantras to invoke devas connected to the elements of fire, water, air, and earth. Many of these mantras are held in secret by shamans, priests, priestesses, and medicine people. They are closely guarded because they can invoke a great deal of power. Like a large surge of electricity passing through an overloaded circuit board, high concentrations of devic energy in the hands of someone who is unprepared to handle it can be very dangerous.

As opposed to attracting devic energy through love and respect, mantras often involve a more mind-focused approach to invocation. Unless we have achieved a high degree of personal integration among our physical, emotional, mental, and spiritual natures, mantric invocations can attract more power than we can safely deal with. In *Letters on Occult Meditation,* Alice Bailey addresses the dangers of invoking devas through specific mantras:

> As may be imagined, the calling of either the devas or the elementals can only be safely undertaken by one who has the power to utilize them wisely when called, hence the mantras we have enumerated above are only put into the hands of those who are on the side of the constructive forces of the system, or who can constructively control the destructive elements, bending them into line with the disintegrating forces that are themselves part of the great constructive scheme. Should anyone—not thus capable—be able to contact the devas, and through the use of mantras gather them to him, he would find that the force they carry would descend on him as a destructive one, and serious consequences might result.

## ATTRACTING NEGATIVITY

On the subject of invoking devic energies, some further words of caution are necessary about dealing with larger amounts of energy and attracting subtler forces to us that are for our good. We mentioned earlier that, as on the physical plane, the subtle planes of existence are populated by a wide variety of living forms. Some are at higher stages of evolution than others, with varying levels of consciousness and integration. As may some human beings, some inhabitants in the subtle planes may try to disguise their true nature, in order to use us for their own purposes.

As with other levels of existence, "like attracts like" on the subtle planes. This means that we often resonate with similar energies in the subtle planes and will attract these energies to us. To the degree that we have not recognized, acknowledged, and integrated the divergent or "shadow" aspects of our nature, we face the danger of attracting negative energies in our work with devas. The love of power (especially psychic power), pride, and separateness are three of the most common problems confronting humanity, which are closely followed by lack of self-esteem, feelings of unworthiness, unresolved sexual issues, and old wounds that have yet to be healed.

Whenever we engage in spiritual practices, we often open ourselves to energies that get pumped into our entire being, including those areas that are divergent or alienated. When it is no longer possible to repress the negativity, it can be destructive. To the degree that we ignore, deny, or avoid our shadow selves, we increase the risk involved in invoking the power of devas.

By acknowledging and welcoming our divergent energies back "into the family," so to speak, we can transform them into their positive components. In addition, the energy that is bound up in denying and suppressing the divergent energy is released and becomes available for more productive activities. At the same time, the self-knowledge that we gain helps protect us from negativity.

The earlier chapters of this book were designed to help develop self-awareness, compassion, and humility. To the extent that we follow a spiritual path grounded in these qualities, we *will naturally resonate with and attract similar energies in the subtler realms of existence.* As a result, we will feel their comfort and support when we invoke devic energies. The love and respect that we emit into the atmosphere is the best protection from negative energies.

In the unlikely event that you attract an energy or spirit being you feel uncomfortable with, ask yourself, "What is it in me that attracts this force?" In such a situation, this supposedly "negative" energy is actually there to help you recognize an alienated aspect of yourself. Whenever you meet such a being or energy in the subtle realms, you need to follow your intuition regarding its intent. If you have any doubts at all, speak from your innermost being, "If you come in the name of God, you are welcome. If not, please go away." This should be followed by a prayer to the Great Spirit or your guardian spirits for protection and clarity.

These cautionary words are not intended to frighten you, nor to prevent you from making contact with nature spirits. By choosing to work in the subtle realms of existence, however, you are entering an unfamiliar world with its own inhabitants, forces, and terrain. By taking the necessary precautions and entering this world with goodwill and respect,

*Maid of the Mist, approaching Niagara Falls*

your journey will unfold naturally and safely through your own inner guidance. You will follow your own spiritual itinerary and create your own unique adventure.

## VISITING PLANETARY POWER SPOTS

Although the techniques offered above can facilitate the invocation of nature spirits on an intimate level, visiting planetary power spots as a spiritual quest poses both unique challenges and unforgettable opportunities.

Because planetary power spots are often popular tourist destinations, a person who makes a solemn pilgrimage to a place like Niagara Falls or the Grand Canyon often will have to deal with busloads of tourists, groups of noisy schoolchildren, and photographers elbowing each other to get the best picture of the waterfall, canyon, or volcano. While each planetary power spot presents a distinct situation, the following guidelines toward invocation may be helpful:

1. Try to make your visit either alone or with people who understand your serious intent (and ideally, who share your desire to commune

with the devas). While most tourists tend to rush their visit, you should devote plenty of time to experience the power spot fully. Be conscious of the fact that you are in an especially sacred and powerful creation of the Earth Mother that is worthy of your time!

For this reason, try if you can to spend at least several days in the vicinity of the power spot. In addition to providing the opportunity for you to enjoy repeated and prolonged visits, you will have time to explore the surrounding area more fully away from the crowds. In an especially vast power spot like Iguassu Falls, many hiking trails away from the primary cataracts allow the visitor to explore the area extensively and experience many kinds of devic energy. Near Niagara Falls, you can have close (and solitary) access to the Niagara River above the falls. There are also hiking trails with access to safe places by the rapids near the whirlpool within a mile downstream. Take advantage of what nature has provided!

2. Although you may not be able to smudge yourself in your hotel room or to leave a lighted candle there while you are gone, take a shower and do your meditation before you venture off. During meditation, ask the primary deva of the power spot for assistance in allowing you to commune with its energy. Strive to maintain your meditative composure as you enter the realm of the devas, even though you may be part of a crowd of tourists.

3. Remember that if you visit a planetary power spot, you will be coming into contact with many different types of nature spirits. In a place like Angel Falls in Venezuela (the highest waterfall in the world), they will include those connected to the mountain, the river, the falls itself, the cliffs, and the winds. Try not to limit your perspective in invoking only one type of deva, even if it is the most obvious one. Be open to all of them!

4. Many people who are sensitive to nature spirits are also sensitive to the energies of other people. For this reason, they often try to avoid crowds. However, if you visit a planetary power spot, lots of fellow humans will likely be there with you also. If this is the case, try to allow the other people present to affect you only in a positive way. Although you may see them all only as "tourists" at first, remember that each individual around you has probably devoted much time, energy, and expense to visit the power spot, which they chose to see instead of visiting a museum or amusement park.

Although they may not realize it on an intellectual level, many people are deeply moved when they are in the presence of powerful devic energy. Accept the diversities among your human companions, and allow yourself to share the feelings of awe, wonder, joy, and excitement that your neighbors are experiencing. Remember that your energetic connection with the devic power can enhance that of your neighbor as well, even if it is not at a conscious level.

5. Take advantage of all possibilities of close devic contact, even if they may appear to be crassly commercial tourist attractions. At Niagara Falls, for example, the popular Cave of the Winds tour and Maid of the Mist boat ride bring you right to the base of the falls. In addition to allowing you to be totally immersed in the winds and the spray, you will also experience the strongest concentrations of devic power.

   Because devic energy often extends hundreds of feet into the atmosphere, helicopter rides are also valuable ways of accessing it. Landing atop Mount Cook in New Zealand, or flying over the Grand Canyon, Iguassu Falls, or the Mauna Loa volcano are not only thrilling excursions you will always remember, but can be powerful spiritual experiences as well.

6. Visiting a planetary power spot during the off-season will probably mean that fewer people will be there. If you cannot travel at this time of the year, you can visit it at an nonpeak hour, usually early in the morning or late in the evening. One of my most memorable experiences at Niagara was to arrive at the Canadian Falls just after midnight during a snowstorm. Being the only human being there allowed me to experience the energy of the falls in a uniquely powerful way.

7. Remember that you do not have to be next to the power spot to access its energy. Since many power spots have become tourist destinations, they are often surrounded by parks and gardens, which are also populated by devas and nature spirits. For instance, if you were to visit the Grand Canyon, you would find many quiet places nearby for meditation or other types of spiritual work. Once you have made initial contact with the devas at the primary power spot, you can maintain this contact consciously even if you were to move a few hundred yards away.

# 9
# Communion

*Let the kingdom of your heart be so wide that no one is excluded.*
**—N. Sri Ram, Thoughts for Aspirants**

Communion with members of the devic kingdom—the sharing of thoughts or feelings with another form of life—does not merely involve the act of receiving, but implies our active participation in a dynamic relationship.

This relationship can take many forms. It is not only based on the "chemistry" between ourselves and the nature being, but on our particular feelings and needs at the time of communion. For example, I mentioned earlier that I often visit a special grove of elm trees near my home for inspiration and guidance. Sometimes, I go there simply to visit the grove. If I happen to be working on a chapter for a book, I often receive guidance concerning my writing. If I am having difficulty with another person, I may receive guidance about the deeper nature of the problem, even if I do not consciously ask for help about it.

Since every human being is complex and unique, each of us will have a different relationship with members of the devic realms. This would hold true even if two close friends with similar interests entered into communion with the same nature spirit. If one of the friends happened to be a scientist and the other an artist, their experience could be dramatically different. This is why two clairvoyants who commune with the same nature being often receive different impressions, and they would both be "right."

We mentioned earlier that not all nature spirits will resonate with us.

While many devas are eager for contact with human beings, some may have other tasks to fulfill and need to be left alone. Very often, the devas that are most receptive to humans are those connected to flowers and trees that were planted by humans, or those that inhabit places where humans visit regularly, like a park, lake, waterfall, or stream. Dora Van Gelder Kunz, a clairvoyant and healer who has communicated with devas for more than eighty years, says that mountain devas in particular have a strong interest in humanity, and are very receptive to communion with us.

Some nature spirits resonate especially well with people in need of healing, while others resonate with those of us requiring inspiration, heightened awareness of nature, or need to access specific knowledge or information.

## WAYS OF COMMUNING WITH DEVAS

### Writing

As a person who enjoys communicating through the written word, I found that the easiest way for me to commune with devas was through "automatic" writing. Automatic writing is nothing more than being in a receptive, meditative state and then instinctively writing down whatever "comes through." I discovered that if I did the preparatory grounding mentioned earlier, I could access information on any subject that interested me.

After you invoke the devas, go into a meditative, receptive state. After several minutes, you may feel a devic presence, which can only be described as an inspiring yet caressing energy. Feel your gratitude to be with the deva. Try to be open to its message without setting your own agenda about what you would like to hear.

With notebook and pen in hand, either ask to be open to the teaching you need to receive, or ask a specific question on any subject of your choosing. When I first began to commune with flower devas, I would simply ask to be open to receive their message, whatever it was. Each message was unique according to either the individual flower or species itself, its location, the role it saw itself as fulfilling in the community, or my particular needs at the time.

One of the most simple yet inspiring messages I received came from

*Wild petunias, Brooklyn, New York*

a deva connected to a wild petunia. It was growing abundantly from a crack in the wall of an old house in the Greenpoint section of Brooklyn:

> Being able to triumph over adversity does not imply surviving—it implies prosperity. You humans create so many limits to your life. Limits regarding love, money, health, intellectual development, happiness, and lasting spiritual unfoldment. You say: "I cannot go further than this." "I am too old." "I am too young." "It's too late." "I'm barely getting by." Limits. Excuses. Closed-mindedness.
>
> It may be true that many of you indeed have a hard path to tread. One of real challenges and limitation. Many of you overcome these challenges, and then believe that your work is over. Yet nine times out of ten it is not over. Nine times out of ten, you need to take the next step and the next and the next. To capitalize, as it were, on your success. To move forward. To use the valuable experience you have gained and put it out into the world. For overcoming obstacles and challenges is your springboard to the next step. The joy, experience, and knowledge you have gained is ready to propel you to the next step.
>
> Please see life in this positive, expansive way. For as you can see, I grow from a tiny crack in the wall. And I am not barely surviving. I am

thriving. So be conscious of the reality of an expanding universe. Learn its laws well, for overcoming adversity is a precious accomplishment; and more precious still if it leads to continued, accelerated expansion and liberation. Liberation from the limits that bind you.

As I continued working with devas in this way, I learned that because they are intimately connected to the Earth Mother, all are potential sources of Earth wisdom. Humans possess this wisdom as well, but often we are cut off from it, especially those of us living in urban environments. Devas assist us not only by imparting this natural wisdom, but by helping us open ourselves to the wisdom within. I soon began consulting the devas on personal issues, environmental questions, writing projects, and specific matters concerning the material to include in this book.

Since most of us are not accustomed to receiving energy from nature beings, many people feel tired after working with them through writing for more than several minutes. When I first began "taking dictation" from devas, I often went from flower garden to flower garden, eager to make their acquaintances and receive their messages. I was excited to work with them, and it seemed that they were very eager to communicate with me, probably because they are usually so ignored by humans. Yet after receiving messages from five or six flower devas in a row, I was exhausted.

One morning, after an especially busy day transcribing messages from the flower devas, I woke up feeing tired and sore. I decided to visit my chiropractor, who himself is sensitive to the subtle realms of nature. After adjusting my spine, he advised: "It's great to commune with flowers, but don't feel that you have to do the whole flower show at once." In other words, it is better to access devic energy in small doses, especially at first. Since that time, I have found that by pacing myself and being sensitive to my own energy level, I am able to communicate with devas for a longer period of time without feeling tired.

## Creating Art

For those who have a gift for artistic creation, drawing, sketching, or painting while in the conscious presence of devas offers both a unique and highly rewarding experience. Since the very keynote of devas is beauty, allowing them to assist us in creating works of beauty is a true act of communion. The following extract was offered by a deva connected with jimsonweed near some train tracks:

*Jimsonweed blossom, Brooklyn, New York*

The beauty that we offer you comes from the depths. It comes from the heart and soul of the Earth Mother. It encompasses all the delicacy, the yearning, and the purpose of the fullest expression of beauty that is known.

Beauty lies deep in the hearts and souls of each of you, my dears, yet it is too often found wanting. It is either completely closed off, or it is expressed in ways that are distorted and grotesque. Has it not been curious to you how humans can create so much beauty and at the same time encounter such ugliness in art, design, architecture, and city planning? The true expression of beauty is often left untapped. In some people it is never manifest at all.

If you are a professional artist, designer, or architect, we only ask that you place the highest priority on beauty. For there is so much ugliness in so many of the modern creations that have been manifest. Creating ugliness from the elements of the Earth Mother—be they of the mineral or plant kingdoms—is insulting. It is insulting to both these elements and to your fellow human beings. . . . So become more aware of beauty: the beauty that you find in the world around you and the beauty that can be found deep within your being.

Although few artists have acknowledged collaborating with devas, a look at many of the inspiring nature paintings of artists like Vincent Van Gogh, Paul Cezanne, and Georgia O'Keefe reveal influences from the subtle realms. The "otherworldly" quality of paintings by the Russian artist and scientist Nicholas Roerich in particular reveal a powerful devic influence, especially in his treatment of light. Roerich also relied on members of the angelic kingdom for guidance in creating his architectural designs, such as the twenty-four-story Master Building in Manhattan, which included a museum, offices, and residences for artists. Now an apartment house, the building was originally designed to include a copper-clad Buddhist stupa at the top.

One of Roerich's favorite places to paint was in the Himalayan mountains. In his book *Himalayas: Abode of Light,* Roerich wrote, "The highest knowledge, the most inspired songs, the most superb sounds and colors are created on the mountains. On the highest mountains there is the Supreme."

Like automatic writing, artistic creation with devas calls on us to be receptive. While there is no need for us to go into a trance, we can allow ourselves to be guided by their wisdom. If you have it in mind to paint a particular tree or landscape, you can allow the resident devas to add a more energetic dimension to your design. If you go to a place in nature with no particular idea of what you are to paint, allow the deva to suggest an appropriate subject. Although it may be on an obvious nature theme, such as a waterfall or the seashore, you may become inspired by the idea of creating a work of art on a more abstract theme like a vortex of energy or the reflection of light on water. Sometimes, devas themselves can appear to people who have the gift of clairvoyant perception, and thus can be a perfect subject for a portrait.

## Sound and Music

Sound is one of the elemental forces in nature; it permeates the entire world. On an elemental level, sound is expressed as waves and vibrations, which often resonate with the energies of devas. When we hear, sound waves traveling through the air resonate in our inner ear. When we speak, we generate sound waves with our larynx. When we play a musical instrument, we create sound vibrations that can stimulate us, relax us, depress us, or lift our spirits.

Like any natural force, sound has the power to build or destroy. In *The Secret Life of Plants,* we read how different types of sound can either stimulate or retard plant growth. The emerging field of music therapy has shown how different types of music can assist in both physical and emotional healing. Merchants have used music for decades to stimulate customer purchases subliminally. By becoming aware of the power of sound and using sound to create harmony in our speech and our music, we can become powerful agents for good in our lives.

Because sound is essentially a subtle form of vibration, it has a powerful effect on devas. In a lecture at Pumpkin Hollow Farm, Dora Van Gelder Kunz related how music can help prepare the atmosphere to attract devas to us and allow them to use the energy of music and distribute it as part of their task of form building and healing. For this reason, the judicious use of music can be used to attract devas, facilitate communion with them, and assist them in their work. The inner realms of music was described by a deva connected to a flower garden at the entrance to a music school:

> Music is a special form of vibration. It is part of the vibration that makes up all life here on Earth. It is, in a sense, akin to us flowers, because music in its highest state can bring you to the roots of your being, to your earthiness, to your natural selves. It can help you rediscover your essential ties to the Earth Mother. Yet music can also bring you to the heights, to the realms of Father Sky.
>
> Music can have a powerful effect on your thoughts. It can help build powerful thought forms of positivity, striving, and organization. It can also help break down old and useless thought forms and attitudes and replace them with the new—or it can simply tear down the old and leave an empty space for the new to begin!
>
> There is no finer music than that which inspires, that brings you up to the heavens. It is music for your soul. Many, many composers throughout the ages have connected with the spiritual dimensions of music and have based their creations on this reality. If you are a composer of music, pray to connect to the spiritual source of musical expression. The beings who reside in the spirit realms will help you gladly and eagerly, for when music is composed and played with the intent to lift the human spirit, it is among the greatest of blessings. It comes directly from the heart of all creation.

We can use music in several ways to attract and commune with devic beings. First, we can play sacred, harmonious, or meditative music on a tape player as we meditate in a grove of trees, by a lake, or in a garden.

In addition to our own focused and sincere intent, the music will help prepare the atmosphere for communion between ourselves and the devic beings.

A more personal method involves creating sound vibrations through chanting and praying. By selecting prayers and chants that uplift the human spirit, we not only attract devas who resonate with this energy, but we open ourselves to communion with them at a higher, more refined level of our being. One would assume that the monks who sing Gregorian or Tibetan tone chants attract many powerful devas to their monastery, and this enables the monks to cocreate with devas in both the physical and superphysical realms.

Singing is another powerful method to attract devas to us and to facilitate communion with them. A friend of mine is an operatic tenor who enjoys singing as he walks through the woods. Once, he sang an aria from an opera that expressed his love of the Great Spirit. His song literally filled the forest and attracted energies around him that could only be described as angelic. The meditative playing of uplifting music on stringed instruments, bells, drums, or woodwinds could have a similar effect.

It is important to point out that since sound is a powerful force, it should always be respected, especially when we engage in spiritual work. Just as meditative music can attract devic beings that resonate with healing, wisdom, and upliftment, discordant sounds can attract elemental energies that thrive on disharmony and divisiveness. As a result, they can strengthen the disharmonious elements within ourselves rather than help us to heal and transform them.

## Communing with Devas in the Garden

The survival of humans is based on foods derived from the plant kingdom. Even if we eat meat, the animals whose flesh we consume all depended on an rich diet of grains, pulses, and grasses in order to achieve slaughter weight. When we look at life from a material dimension only, it would appear that through planting seeds and providing them with water, fertilizer, and chemical insecticides, we will continue to be fed on the material level.

Over the years, however, a growing number of farmers and small-scale gardeners have realized that in addition to the fiber, protein, vitamins, and minerals we receive from our food, we also receive its life force with the subtle energies it imparts. In addition to acknowledging and honoring this life force through praying before a meal, many have recognized the importance of acknowledging this life energy—as coordinated through devic beings—when we cultivate fruits, vegetables, and grains for ourselves and other members of our community. Writing in *The Theosophist,* L. E. Girard observed:

> If grain is sown and cultivated without thinking of the life which gives it being, that life, being unstimulated to higher things, merely fulfills its own law of being. But when the cultivator understands that every grain possessing germinal tendencies can be made to react to special influence, he is able to bring about two real and useful results which, added to the fine body of crops resulting from scientific agriculture, produces superior food.
>
> The two results are these: first, that by intelligently appealing to the forces of nature the cultivator invites into his field hosts of Nature Spirits of the most beautiful and varied kind, which assist him in the growing of plants; second, that they contribute to that growth a life-side that they alone can give.

Communion with landscape and garden devas presents a special opportunity, because it is by necessity an ongoing cocreative relationship: We are involved in assisting the devas in the creation of life through working with the elements. For this reason, great sensitivity is necessary in order to be receptive to their guidance on how we can best help them achieve nature's fullest expression. Rather than insisting on running the show, as humans normally do when planning and cultivating a garden, we are humbly striving to collaborate with the resident devas and nature spirits.

Perhaps the best-known example of human-deva cooperation involves Eileen and Peter Caddy, Dorothy Maclean, and others at the renowned Findhorn Garden in Scotland. By following the advice of the devas connected to both the local landscape and different species of plants, they were able to grow a magnificent garden on desertlike soil. In the classic book *The Findhorn Garden,* Dorothy Maclean related the devas' perspective on what a garden really is:

> To a deva, the garden is not an assembly of forms and colors but rather moving lines of energy. In describing our garden they said they could see the forces from below gradually being drawn up and blending with those coming down in great, swift waves. Within this field of energy, each plant was an individual whirlpool of activity.

By working with devas, the human residents at Findhorn not only received deep spiritual insights, but practical knowledge regarding planting, composting, and plant care. Peter Caddy spoke about his early experiences in *The Findhorn Garden:*

> They told us how far apart plants should be, how often to water them, what was wrong and what to do about it. . . . For example, after I had sown our first lettuce seeds, I did as the garden books advised, thinning the rows and planting out the thinnings to make five or six rows out of the original one. But most of our transplanted leaves started dying, and we didn't know why. When Dorothy asked the Lettuce Deva what to do, we were told it would be better to sow seeds thickly in each row, then eliminate those that are weak, rather than transplant. We could recycle the life force in them through the compost. This proved to be sound advice.

Different people will commune with nature spirits in their own unique way. While Dorothy Maclean has the ability to "listen" to the devas and record their works on paper, many gardeners work with devas subconsciously. Although they may not even be aware of the fact that they are working with the devic realms, they always have an intuitive sense of what is needed to create a beautiful and healthy garden. We all know of people who possess the proverbial "green thumb" and who always cultivated the healthiest, most beautiful gardens. Many of these gardeners talk to their plants and send them good feelings. While not consciously aware that they are communing with nature spirits, many gardeners experience a sense of peace and centeredness when working with plants. In their book *The Experience of Nature,* Rachel Kaplan and Stephen Kaplan address some of the psychological aspects of gardening:

> Gardening provides various means of connectedness, thus enhancing the sense of extent. Some may experience in gardening a historical connection, a tie to former times and generations past. Certainly, many gardeners feel a relationship to a force or system that is larger than they are and that is not under human control.

## Creating a Garden

If you are interested in creating a garden, do the preparatory work mentioned earlier. Go to the area where you wish to plant, present your offerings to the devas, and invoke their presence in a way that manifests your respect and gratitude for their important work. I have found that Geoffrey Hodson's invocation mentioned in the previous chapter is especially useful at this time.

You may wish to have paper and pencil in hand in order to receive guidance regarding the garden's design. After you have performed the invocations offered in the previous chapter, survey the area where you would like the garden to be. It may be at present an open natural space, or it may have been the location of a garden at an earlier time. View this natural space with reverence, knowing that the growth of plants for human food and enjoyment is a unique gift of the Earth Mother. In Machaelle Small Wright's *Perelandra Garden Workbook*, the importance of the energetic component of a garden was described by the Perelandra Garden deva as going beyond creating higher quality food:

> The direction of vibrant, life-giving energy not only moves into the plants and their vegetables. It also radiates out from the garden into the surrounding land and impacts all form within that area. Perhaps it would be easier to visualize what we are saying if one saw the garden as an energy generator.

Humans often prefer planting creating gardens in the form of a square or rectangle. When we wish to collaborate with devas, however, we need to be open to the possibility of cocreating a garden in the form of a circle, an oval, or an irregular shape that is in harmony with the contours of the land. We can also be guided regarding how many rows to make in the garden, as well as their proper width and depth.

We then need to know what types of plants we wish to cultivate. Of course, some intellectual knowledge is required here; if we live in a northern climate, trying to grow plants that thrive in the tropics is often doomed to failure, no matter how close our relationship with a deva might be. After we have a general idea of what we would like to plant, we can ask the deva for guidance regarding our selections. Using the method of writing mentioned earlier, you can simply ask the deva which seeds to plant and write them down in your notebook. Be prepared to receive information that you may not have considered before; for example, the deva may suggest that you plant certain flowers alongside the vegetables. You can also ask a specific question requiring a "yes" or "no" answer, such as, "Should I plant tomatoes?"

One method of communion with garden devas is through dowsing.

According to Patricia C. and Richard D. Wright in *The Divining Heart*, dowsing is defined as "the process of discovering or uncovering information through the medium of the self." Dowsing is an ancient form of divination, often done using a light branch of hazel or willow in the shape of the letter Y. Dowsing can also be done with a pendulum on a string, easily found in metaphysical and New Age bookshops. This method is especially useful for individuals who do not yet totally trust their intuition when they work with devic energies. The technique for pendulum dowsing is very simple: While holding the pendulum suspended over the seeds or baby plants, you ask questions that require a "yes" or "no" answer.

You need first to establish what signifies a "yes" or a "no." For example, you can ask, "What constitutes a 'yes'?" and the pendulum may either swing back and forth or move in a circle. If, for instance, you have established that a "yes" involves the pendulum swinging back and forth, a "no" would be indicated by the pendulum moving in a circle. You may then ask the landscape devas specific questions on any subject, as long as they require a "yes" or "no" answer. For example, you can ask the deva, "Should I plant cucumbers?" and depending on how the pendulum moves, you will have an answer. You can continue to ask questions in this way as you design and plant the garden, as well as when you are actively cultivating it. You can ask specific questions about fertilizing, weeding, thinning, and watering, as well as queries regarding insects and other visitors.

While many people like to cultivate all available land, residents of Findhorn learned of the importance of keeping a corner of their garden wild, where the devas could live and work without human interference. By doing so, they recognized the spiritual force in "wild" nature, and honored the devic presences in a most respectful way.

If you are serious about working with garden devas, the *Perelandra Garden Workbook* is the most comprehensive guide available (see Resources). Written by a woman who has communed and co-created with garden devas for more than ten years, the workbook provides detailed information regarding both the outer and inner aspects of planning and cultivating a garden in collaboration with devas and nature spirits.

## Working with Herbs

Because humans have been using herbal remedies for thousands of years, shamans and other healers have been in touch with devic consciousness on a subconscious level throughout human history. Today, modern herbalists consciously work with devas to gain knowledge of the medicinal qualities of herbs, as well as to determine the proper dosages and uses for individual needs. Dorothy Maclean records a deva's explanation that plants such as herbs, which have long associations with humans, "are thus ready to be leaders in the cooperation between our two worlds. We are part of human consciousness."

Like the gardener, the herbalist can center herself before going to commune with the herb in a quiet state of meditation. She may ask a general question like "What are the essential qualities that you impart?" Pen in hand, she would then remain in receptive silence and intuitively receive and write down the information the herb deva may have to share with her.

She may also use a pendulum to ask the herb deva a specific question that requires a "yes" or "no" answer, such as a question regarding the proper use or dosage of an herb. For example, if she wants to know, "Are two servings of peppermint tea the proper dosage for this patient?" she can hold the pendulum over some peppermint and ask "yes" or "no" questions regarding proper dosage. She should continue to ask the question until it is answered:

"Is one serving the proper dosage?" (no)
"Are two servings the proper dosage?" (yes)
"Are three servings the proper dosage?" (no)

In this case, the correct answer would be "two."

## PLANTING A SACRED GROVE

The concept of planting a sacred grove of trees goes back to the beginnings of human civilization and was common among the ancient Greeks, Egyptians, Romans, and especially among the Druids. It is still very appropriate for today's environmental consciousness, however, since trees are so vital for a healthy planet. Sacred groves can be used to commemorate a birth, a rite of passage, a marriage, an anniversary, a death, a particular success, or a personal wish or aspiration. As a home for devic beings, a grove can also serve as a sanctuary and a place for healing, transformation, or lifelong learning.

Designing a sacred grove can be accomplished with the assistance of the resident landscape devas. By allowing them to help us see the situation from *their* point of view, they can help us to intuitively sense where the grove should be planted, thus increasing the energy of the particular spot. They will also help us become more conscious of the type of energy we would like the sacred grove to create, determined by the species of tree we are to plant. Shamans, magicians, and priests have often been responsible for the creation of sacred groves, working with the devas in locating the groves and in choosing the appropriate types of trees to plant in them.

By studying both the biology and lore of different tree species, we can become more aware of the physical, mystical, and symbolic qualities that a tree possesses. This may help us select from several tree species that have a reputation for healing (such as the elder) or those connected to wisdom (like the oak). Some people may wish to plant trees that trace their lineage to famous and historic trees.

The exact placement of trees is important. We must make sure that the space for planting is the correct size and depth, that the drainage of the soil is adequate for the species, and that the trees are planted a proper distance from each other. In addition to relying on our educated intelligence based on knowledge or training, asking the devas for their advice is especially helpful at this stage.

Knowing how to look after the trees we plant is important as well, both for the trees' sake as well as our own as custodians of these young trees. As with a garden, the resident devas can assist us in caring for the newly planted trees. Weed control, composting, providing adequate water, occasional pruning, providing first aid, and protecting trees from animals and human vandalism all require our active participation during the first few years of a tree's life. Nurturing a tree in this way can be a tremendous pleasure and is an expression of our concern for the Earth and the other forms of life that share the planet with us.

## SUPERCONSCIOUS CONSERVATION

Active communion with devas and nature spirits will also help heal an often-ravaged environment. Whenever we decide to initiate or participate in projects to restore eroded landscapes, clean up a polluted or trash-filled area, plant an area with trees and shrubs, create green spaces or build "vest-pocket" parks in an urban environment, we are working with the creative energies of the resident devic presences. By being receptive to their inspiration and wisdom, we set aside our human egos and seek to understand the situation from the devic point of view. As a result, we are not only assisting them in their valuable work, but we are cocreating with them on both obvious and subtle levels.

# CONTEMPLATION

While some people commune with devas through writing, music, or art, or through gardening or planting trees, the vast majority of us will commune with devas on subconscious levels. Aside from feelings of comfort, inspiration, and well-being, we may not even be aware that we are communing with them. This does not mean that we are doing anything wrong or that we are less spiritually evolved than people who can see devas or communicate with them consciously in the garden. It merely means that at this particular time, subconscious (or unconscious) communion is more appropriate for us. For some people, receiving devic wisdom at a subconscious level may even be far more valuable and lasting than information received by the conscious mind.

In a society where one's outer status is often paramount, it can be difficult for us to value private, inner experiences that are not outwardly obvious. Yet by seeing validity in our personal experiences, we are more able to fully experience the blessings that communion with devas has to offer.

Whether we can see the devas through clairvoyant sight or perceive their wisdom on a subconscious level, the true value of our communion with them is felt in the impact it has on our lives and is demonstrated by the extent to which we apply our understanding to assist in the process of planetary healing.

# I O

# Healing

*Help Nature and work on with her; and Nature will regard thee as*
*one of her creators and make obeisance. And she will open wide*
*before thee the portals of her secret chambers.*
**—H.P. Blavatsky, The Voice of the Silence**

The word "heal" traces its roots to the Anglo-Saxon *hal*, which means "whole," "hale," or "hearty." Healing involves root concepts like wholeness, wellness, and integration. In Native American terms, it means "walking in balance on the Earth Mother."

Healing is the essence of life itself. Without healing, there would be no possibility of evolution. As a living being, the Earth is a self-healing entity. She works to realign energies, and she adjusts aspects of herself that are out of harmony and out of alignment. The process of healing has been a constant process since the birth of the planet. And despite the increasing ravages done to the Earth by human beings, the healing process will continue. The larger question is whether humanity will continue to participate in the Earth's healing process or whether we will destroy ourselves through pollution, disease, or the unwise use of the Earth's resources.

By learning how to commune and work with the subtle forces of nature, we can learn how assist in the Earth's preservation. As we become actively involved in planetary healing, we also participate in our own.

## HEALING OURSELVES

Many of humanity's oldest healing traditions—including chi gong, ayurveda, acupuncture, laying on of hands, visiting hot springs and mineral springs, crystal healing, and herbalism—work with the Earth's innate healing energies to assist us in our personal healing process. Even in modern allopathic medicine, which is presently the dominant form of curing in the Western industrialized nations, many commercial medications are derived from trees, herbs, and other plants.

When we seek to commune with the Earth Mother personally, however, we open ourselves to her healing power more directly. When we come to visit any living form, whether that form is a waterfall, a river, a tree, or an open field of flowers, we are communing with the intelligence and living force that stand behind its evolution. As a result, we open ourselves to a powerful source of healing energy. Because nature is the harmonious and cooperative alignment of all the elements of creation, nature is the ultimate healer affecting all aspects of our being.

The healing of the Earth is undertaken to a large extent by members of the devic kingdom. By assisting in the processes of alignment, growth, replacement, readjustment, and protection, devas and nature spirits work to heal the planet. Although they perform their tasks at different intensities and in different planes, their healing work is performed all the time, day and night.

Human beings are an integral part of nature's family, and it is part of our human birthright to access the devas' healing powers whenever we need to. By coming into contact with natural forms, we are able to acknowledge the alienated aspects of our being, integrate our own divergent energies, and align ourselves with the natural forces around us in the rest of the natural world.

After communing with a deva connected to the Raymond's Kill waterfall near Milford, Pennsylvania, I was left with the impression that being able to access the tremendous healing powers of nature is not only an essential aspect of human-deva communion but the major part of our subconscious work with them. Since healing is a power inherent in all living beings, we not only possess the inner power to heal ourselves, but we resonate with this same power that dwells in all other living beings. Devas not only resonate with our innate healing power, but they are able to penetrate the energetic blockages that contribute to states of ill health—whether mental, physical, or psychological.

Nature spirits can resonate with the aspect in us that needs to be healed on the most subtle energetic levels. For example, if our health problem is primarily a result of wrong thinking, stuck attitudes, limited perspectives, or holding on to old concepts we no longer need, devas can inspire within us, in a subtle way, the reality of a changing universe; the need to be open, to change, to transform, to look higher, to move ahead in our life, or to perceive the reality that lies behind the form.

If our state of illness is due to past hurts that have not yet been resolved, devas can gently offer their healing power that resonates with our "inner healer." This can help us resolve old hurts in a way that is best for us. Very often, healing does not work on a logical, mental level; the subtle healing of an old hurt (even one that we may not have been previously conscious of) can awaken or unblock our innate healer within and lead to recovery.

Our ill health may be due to an energetic lack of some kind. Being in contact with a source of healing energy, like a waterfall, river, lake, or ocean, can offer us the additional energy we need to enhance our own healing process. By learning how to access the healing energy of devas, we can increase our overall energy level.

## ACCESSING HEALING ENERGY

When you visit a place for healing, pay your respects to the deva, make an offering if you wish, make your prayers to facilitate resonance, and become receptive to the powerful energies that are available for your use.

It is also important to *ask* for healing; you can actively state the outer problem, or the inner problem if you know it. Ask to be healed *if it is God's will.* Asking for healing power according to the will of God or in the name of the Great Spirit will provide you with a safe amount of healing energy that will neither be too much nor too little; it is best to simply ask for the healing power you need to enable you to heal yourself. Do not set a specific mental agenda about what constitutes healing, because healing may need to take place on more than the physical level. In some cases physical healing may not be possible, while emotional healing is. Be open to the process of healing in whatever direction it may take. Healing implies learning, patience, alignment, and resolution.

You may wish to invoke the healing energy of the devas on some other person's behalf—a person who may not be consciously communing with devas. At this point, you may wish to use a healing prayer to invoke the presence of the devas who specialize in healing. Many have utilized the rather formal invocation that was given to Geoffrey Hodson by devic beings more than sixty years ago and published in *The Brotherhood of Angels and of Men:*

*Hail devas of the Healing Art!*
*Come to our aid.*
*Pour forth your healing life into (this person).*
*Let every cell be charged anew with Vital Force.*
*To every nerve give peace.*
*Let tortured sense be soothed.*
*May the rising tide of life set every limb aglow*
*As, by your healing power,*
*Both soul and body are restored.*
*Leave here (or there) an angel watcher,*
*To comfort and protect,*
*Till health returns or life departs,*
*That he may ward away all ill,*
*May hasten the returning strength—*
*Or lead to peace when life is done.*
*Hail, devas of the healing art!*
*Come to our aid,*
*And share with us the labors of this earth,*
*That God may be set free in man.*

The healing process does not only involve the removal of outer symptoms. True healing requires alignment. It calls for us to align our beliefs, emotions, and energies to the will of God and also to the rhythm of the Earth Mother herself. Of course, this process will require some effort on your part; you must act on the new insights and discoveries that may be presented to you during the initial healing process. For example, if being in a hurtful relationship is a factor in your lack of alignment or harmony, you may need to change or end/leave the relationship. In many cases the healing process may involve making difficult or even painful decisions.

As a son or daughter of the Earth Mother, and as a human relative to nature beings or devas, nature's healing power is there for each of us, as a gift with no strings attached. It is part of the "savings account" that we bring into the world when we are born. The only limitations to healing are those that we place on it through being cut off from nature on mental, emotional, physical, spiritual, and energetic levels. One deva asked the question, "Is it no wonder, therefore, that as a race of beings, you humans are so sick? So sick on all levels of your being?"

Different nature beings offer specific keynote or essential qualities that are inherent in their nature or with the type of nature form they are connected with—such as water (moving or still), trees, rocks, winds, or

*Laja Waterfall, Chile*

fire—and certain subtle forces of nature will resonate especially with you. For example, I have discovered that I resonate best with the energies of the mountains and winds. Going to a windy place or a mountaintop would be recommended for my healing. But very often, certain places in nature—such as a waterfall or the seashore—may be the home of several nature spirits with a number of core essences. They can provide a potent *combination* of resonant energies that can help facilitate our healing process. After meditating under Raymond's Kill Falls (and taking a swim in its icy water), I received the following message:

> I am the harmonious convergence of energies involving cliff, moving water, and wind, and to a lesser degree, trees. The power of the moving water involves energy and cleansing from the dense physical to the most subtle spiritual levels. The devas associated with the cliffs offer strength, stability, and the potential of energy yet to be released. The tree devas offer the essence of growth and of living in your vertical nature—connected both to the Earth and the heavens, serving as a bridge and an energy conduit between them. The wind devas offer change; they facilitate communication between the different realms of nature and bring you new ideas and perspectives. (If you are fortunate, you may also access the healing of the rainbow, which touches your innermost soul and helps to purify and refine your most spiritually aligned energies.) So choosing a waterfall to access healing energy is a wise idea, because you can exponentially increase, in a very dynamic and powerful way, the possibility of communion between nature and so many aspects of your being—all at once!

## ELEMENTAL RESONANCE

An important yet often overlooked aspect of healing involves the elemental biological and chemical resonance we experience with other forms of nature. Old scientific thought has separated the world into different species, genera, and kingdoms, which stresses our differences as opposed to focusing on what we have in common. After communing with a deva connected to a cliff near the town of Peulla, Chile, however, I realized that the division of nature into three distinct and separate (animal, plant, and mineral) "kingdoms" is an illusion. All of the natural world is related as *one kingdom*. Although a human being and a cliff are vastly different

*Yellow beech tree, near Pucón, Chile*

*The Pacific Ocean, Pacific Grove, California*

in appearance and expression, the cliff is an aspect of a living planet with a distinct role to play in the evolutionary scheme.

All members of the Earth community—whether human, plant, ocean, or rock—share elements in common. When we eat an orange, for example, we integrate the fruit of a plant into our bodies; the tree that grew the fruit received its nourishment from the minerals and water in the soil. This plant and mineral material becomes our flesh and bone in addition to providing us with the life force we need for survival. And when we die, our body returns these minerals and other organic matter to the soil once again. This "common ground" creates a conscious resonance with the rest of nature that is an important source of healing—whether that healing comes through direct devic energy or through flower essences, medicinal plants, or essential oils.

## HEALING THE PLANET

Nick Gordon, the president of Emissaries Foundation, says that, "In community, I feel that we are each other's medicine." He means that not only do we help heal each other by sharing our gifts of individuality, but we contribute to the healing of the Earth through active involvement with the larger world community. According to Donald M. Epstein in *The Twelve Stages of Healing:*

> The spiritual aspect of healing involves tapping into the deeper levels of being where our innate intelligence resides. As we connect to our inner rhythms and greater sense of wholeness, we begin to experience the rhythms, wholeness, and interconnectedness around us, which eventually expands to include the entire human and planetary community.

As we learn to heal ourselves, we naturally seek to promote healing around us. This idea resonates with that of Native American shamans, who taught that all aspects of nature are dependent on each other. Just as we depend on the Earth Mother, she also depends on humanity. While the Earth heals us, we can assist in healing the Earth. It is a vital aspect of our task as members of the planetary community.

Each individual human being possesses unique gifts, which are a natural expression of who we are. As a result, each of us is naturally drawn to different areas of interest. Our major task is to recognize where our true passions lie and strive to manifest them in the larger community.

On a basic level, we must learn how to "walk lightly" on the Earth. In a society that places a high value on material possessions, it is often difficult to keep a clear perspective on our real needs as opposed to perceived needs. For many people, even the basic needs of clothing, food, and shelter become distorted. We consume food when we aren't really hungry, we have clothes in our closets that we never (or rarely) wear, and we seem to think a house is not a home without appliances, electronic equipment, motor vehicles, furniture, and other objects we really do not need or rarely use. Money—or "green energy"—is often hoarded for the sake of making more money and is not based on any concrete need.

Eating low on the food chain, recycling cans, bottles, and paper, composting, conserving energy and shifting to renewable energy sources, limiting our purchases to what we really need, and investing our money in companies that are sensitive to the needs of the planet will not only help heal the Earth, but will also allow us to become increasingly more sensitive to her needs. While we cannot support every single environmental organization, we can channel our energy (green or otherwise) toward those organizations and groups whose goals and activities are in harmony with our own. The daily expression of sensitivity and respect creates a resonance in ourselves that devas like to respond to.

Preserving the forests is of paramount concern to me. Their protection and preservation is crucial not only because of their environmental value, but because they are an important source of spiritual wisdom and energy that the planet needs for her survival. During a visit to the beautiful Monteverde Cloud Forest Preserve in Costa Rica, I felt that the forest embodied the essence of what a sacred natural temple would be. While meditating in a windy place on the path to Peñas Blancas, I was inspired to write the following impressions in my notebook:

> Unlike your constructed places of worship, this forest is a living temple in every sense of the word. While beauty, power, and peace can be found in a church, a synagogue, or a mosque, you cannot compare it with the presence of God that you can experience here.
>
> So many religions seek to preserve their temples, and members of the respective congregations offer their time, money, and energy for their preservation. By preserving your temples, you preserve a sanctuary that is so important for your spiritual life. And you wish to have this temple serve the coming generations and thus strengthen their link with the Creator.
>
> It is even more important for you to save living temples such as this one—a forest that offers you literally everything a body and soul could want: oxygen, water, beauty, and shelter; healing, power, upliftment, and peace. This forest offers you the closest of links with the beings of the spirit realms, the shining ones, the devas. It also offers you the all-encompassing presence of the Great Spirit.
>
> Yet it takes money to preserve the forests. It takes energy to oversee our protection. It takes intelligence and awareness to understand the workings of nature in a forest system such as this.
>
> I ask you to find how you can help to preserve both this temple and other such temples throughout the world. See how you can help through sharing your energy. Donate money to groups which help preserve and expand the forests. Learn about the forests and the beings who inhabit them. Tell others of your experiences here so that they can savor them as well. See what you can do to aid in our protection and preservation.

# EVER-EXPANDING PERSPECTIVES

We can change our perspectives and open ourselves to the possibilities that communion with nature can provide. As children of the Earth Mother and as members of the Earth family, we are part of the "bigger planetary picture." As a living, breathing part of the Earth, we innately know the secrets that are part of the essence of the Earth. We *already know* what both ourselves and the Earth Mother need for healing; the answers are within, although we may need to be reminded of them at times!

Like all living beings, our planetary home is constantly changing. Change, transition, and transformation are essential aspects of a living process. By becoming grounded, and by working with the nature beings on the subtle planes of existence, we gradually become more aware of these Earth rhythms, Earth wisdom, and Earth transitions—and of our own rhythms, wisdom, and transitions.

Living reality is always a *changing* reality. When we embrace the reality of change, we become more open to what the "now moment" has to teach us. As we deepen our connections with nature and actively involve ourselves in the ongoing process of learning, working, and healing, we begin to participate in a benign cycle: a continual spiral movement of expanded perspectives, deeper understanding, alignment, integration, and active healing.

> *O Hidden Life Vibrant in Every Atom*
> *O Hidden Light, Shining in Every Creature*
> *O Hidden Love, Embracing All in Oneness.*
> *May each of us who feels as One with Thee*
> *Know that we are therefore One with every other.*
> *PEACE TO ALL BEINGS.*

# Reference Bibliography

## Chapter 1

Godwin, Malcolm. *Angels: An Endangered Species.* New York: Simon & Schuster, 1990.

Gold, Peter. *Navajo and Tibetan Sacred Wisdom: The Circle of the Spirit.* Rochester, Vt.: Inner Traditions, 1994.

Hodson, Geoffrey. *Clairvoyant Investigations.* Wheaton, Ill.: Quest Books, 1987.

————. *The Kingdom of the Gods.* Adyar, India: The Theosophical Publishing House, 1970.

————. *Man's Supersensory and Spiritual Powers.* Adyar, India: The Theosophical Publishing House, 1964.

Kunz, Dora Van Gelder. *Angels and Devas.* Audiotape. Craryville, N.Y.: Pumpkin Hollow Farm, n.d.

Lattimore, Richmond, trans. *The Odyssey of Homer.* New York: HarperCollins, 1975.

Lawlor, Robert. *Voices of the First Day.* Rochester, Vt.: Inner Traditions, 1991.

Parisen, Maria, ed. *Angels & Mortals: Their Co-Creative Power.* Wheaton, Ill.: Quest Books, 1990.

Ponce, Charles. *Kabbalah.* Wheaton, Ill.: Quest Books, 1978.

Smith, Joseph, Jr., trans. *The Book of Mormon.* Salt Lake City: The Church of Jesus Christ of Latter-day Saints, 1985.

Southern Centre of Theosophy. *Devas and Men.* Adyar, India: The Theosophical Publishing House, 1977.

Steiner, Rudolf. *The Mission of the Archangel Michael.* Spring Valley, N.Y.: The Anthrosophic Press, 1961.

Wright, Machaelle Small, trans. *Co-Creative Definitions Dealing with Nature, Life, Science, the Universe and All Else.* Warrenton, Va.: Perelandra, Ltd., 1990. Monograph.

———. *Perelandra Garden Workbook.* Jeffersonton, Va.: Perelandra, Ltd., 1987.

## Chapter 2

Altman, Nathaniel. *Sacred Trees.* San Francisco: Sierra Club Books, 1994.

Bolívar Arostegui, Natalia. *Los orishas en Cuba.* Havana: Ediciones Unión, 1990.

Bondi, Julia, with Nathaniel Altman. *Lovelight.* New York: Pocket Books, 1989.

Buck, Peter (Te Rangi Hiroa). *The Coming of the Maori.* Wellington: Whitcombe and Tombs, 1974.

Cabrera, Lydia. *El Monte.* Miami: Ediciones Universal, 1992.

Densmore, Frances. "Notes on the Indians' Belief in the Friendliness of Nature." *Southwestern Journal of Anthropology* 4 (1948).

Devall, Bill, and George Sessions. *Deep Ecology.* Salt Lake City: Peregrine Smith Books, 1985.

Eliade, Mircea, ed. *The Encyclopedia of Religion.* Vol. 15. New York: Macmillan, 1987.

Green, Marian. *The Elements of Natural Magic.* Rockport, Mass.: Element Books, 1989.

Grimal, Pierre, ed. *Larousse World Mythology.* New York: G. P. Putnam's Sons, 1965.

Hastings, James, ed. *Encyclopaedia of Religion and Ethics.* Vol. 9. New York: Charles Scribner's Sons, n.d.

Hodson, Geoffrey. *The Brotherhood of Angels and of Men.* London: The Theosophical Publishing House, 1957.

———. *Clairvoyant Investigations.* Wheaton, Ill.: Quest Books, 1987.

———. *The Kingdom of the Gods.* Adyer, India: The Theosophical Publishing House, 1970.

Hultkranz, Ake. *Belief and Worship in Native North America.* New York: Syracuse University Press, 1981.

King, Serge. *Kahuna Healing.* Wheaton, Ill.: Quest Books, 1983.

Kunz, Dora Van Gelder. *Devic Consciousness.* Craryville, N.Y.: Pumpkin Hollow Farm, 1989.

Lake, Robert (Medicine Grizzlybear). "Power Centers," *The Quest* 2 (Winter 1989).

Larrington, Carolyne, ed. *The Feminist Companion to Mythology.* New York: Pandora Press, 1992.

Lawlor, Robert. *Voices of the First Day.* Rochester, Vt.: Inner Traditions, 1991.

Leadbeater, C. W., *The Hidden Side of Things.* Adyar: The Theosophical Publishing House, 1954.

Maclean, Dorothy. *To Honor the Earth.* San Francisco: HarperSanFrancisco, 1991.

Mercatante, Anthony S. *The Facts on File Encyclopedia of World Mythology and Legend.* New York: Facts on File, 1988.

Mora Penroz, Ziley. *Verdades Mapuches de alta magia para reencantar la tierra de Chile.* Temuco: Editorial Kushe, 1989.

Parisen, Maria, ed. *Angels and Mortals: Their Co-Creative Power.* Wheaton, Ill.: Quest Books, 1990.

Paulson, Ivar. *Old Estonian Folk Religion.* Bloomington: Indiana University Press, 1971.

Piggott, Stuart. *The Druids.* London: Thames and Hudson, 1975.

Rosa, José Alberto, and Nathaniel Altman. *Finding Your Personal Power Spots.* London: Aquarian Press, 1986.

Sheehan, Molly. *A Guide to Green Hope Farm: Flower Essences.* Meriden, N.H.: Green Hope Farm, 1994.

Swan, James A. *The Power of Place.* Wheaton, Ill.: Quest Books, 1991.

Wright, Machaelle Small. *Perelandra Garden Workbook.* Jeffersonton, Va.: Perelandra, Ltd., 1987.

## Chapter 3

Gaines, David, ed. *Mono Lake Guidebook.* Lee Vining, Calif.: Mono Lake Committee, 1989.

Devall, Bill, and George Sessions. *Deep Ecology.* Salt Lake City: Peregrine Smith Books, 1985.

Harman, Willis W. "The Transpersonal Challenge to the Scientific Paradigm: The Need for a Restructuring of Science." *ReVISION* 11, no. 2 (Fall 1988): 13–21.

Lawlor, Robert. *Voices of the First Day.* Rochester, Vt.: Inner Traditions, 1991.

Nichols, Ross. *The Book of Druidry.* Wellingborough: Aquarian Press, 1990.

Rosa, José Alberto, and Nathaniel Altman. *Finding Your Personal Power Spots.* London: Aquarian Press, 1983.

Sheldrake, Rupert. *The Rebirth of Nature.* New York: Bantam Books, 1991.

## Chapter 4

Bailey, Alice. *Glamour: A World Problem.* New York: Lucis Publishing Co., 1950.

Capra, Fritjof. *The Turning Point.* New York: Simon & Schuster, 1982.

Hodson, Geoffrey. *The Kingdom of the Gods.* Adyar, India: The Theosophical Publishing House, 1970.

La Rotta, Constanza, et al. *Especies Utilizadas por la Comunidad Miraña.* Bogota: FEN, n.d.

Lawlor, Robert. *Voices of the First Day.* Rochester, Vt.: Inner Traditions, 1991.

Morley, Sylvester M., and Olivia Gilliam, eds. *Respect for Life.* New York: Myrin Institute Books, 1974.

Pavlik, Bruce M. et al. *Oaks of California.* Los Olivas, Calif.: Cachume Press, 1991.

Perkins, John. *The World Is As You Dream It.* Rochester, Vt.: Destiny Books, 1994.

Swan, James A. *The Power of Place.* Wheaton, Ill.: Quest Books, 1991.

## Chapter 5

Altman, Nathaniel. *The Nonviolent Revolution.* Shaftsbury, England: Element Books, 1989.

Devall, Bill, and George Sessions. *Deep Ecology.* Salt Lake City: Peregrine Smith Books, 1985.

Foster, Steven, and Meredith Little. *The Book of the Vision Quest.* New York: Prentice Hall Press, 1987.

Green, Marian. *The Elements of Natural Magic.* Rockport, Mass.: Element Books, 1989.

Jain, Champat Rai. *Fundamentals of Jainism.* Meerut, India: Veer Nirvan Bharti, 1974.

Joy, Charles R., ed. *Albert Schweitzer: An Anthology.* Boston: The Beacon Press, 1947.

Laxmansurishverji, Vijaya. *Atma Tatva Vichar.* Bombay: Damji Jethabhai, 1963.

Macquarrie, Kim. *Spirits of the Rainforest.* Discovery Communications, Inc., 1993. Video.

Morley, Sylvester M., and Olivia Gilliam, eds. *Respect for Life.* New York: Myrin Institute Books, 1974.

Parry, Danaan, and Lila Forest. *The Earthsteward's Handbook.* Cooperstown, N.Y.: Sunstone Publications, 1987.

Seed, John, et al. *Thinking Like a Mountain.* Philadelphia: New Society Publishers, 1988.

## Chapter 6

Beck, Peggy V., et al. *The Sacred.* Flagstaff, Ariz.: Northland Publishing Co., 1990.

Day, Rick. *Newsletter of the Center for the Living Force.* September, 1975.

Hammarskjold, Dag. *Markings.* London: Faber & Faber, 1964.

Lau, D. C., trans. *Tao Te Ching.* Baltimore: Penguin Books, 1963.

Nasr, Seyyed Hossein. *Man and Nature.* London: Mandala, 1990.

Perlin, John. *A Forest Journey.* Cambridge, Mass.: Harvard University Press, 1989.

## Chapter 7

Bondi, Julia, and Nathaniel Altman. *Lovelight.* New York: Pocket Books, 1989.

Eliade, Mircea, ed. *The Encyclopedia of Religion.* Vol. 8. New York: Macmillan, 1987.

Gold, Peter. *Navajo and Tibetan Sacred Wisdom: The Circle of the Spirit.* Rochester, Vt.: Inner Traditions, 1994.

Harner, Michael. *The Way of the Shaman.* New York: Bantam Books, 1982.

Hastings, John, ed. *Encyclopaedia of Religion and Ethics.* Vol. 9. New York: Charles Scribner's Sons, n.d.

Leach, Marjorie. *Guide to the Gods.* Santa Barbara: ABC-CLIO, 1992.

Lurker, Manfred. *Dictionary of Gods and Goddesses, Devils and Demons.* London: Routledge, 1988.

Rosa, José Alberto, with Nathaniel Altman. *Finding Your Personal Power Spots.* London: Aquarian Press, 1983.


## Chapter 8

Bailey, Alice. *Letters on Occult Meditation.* New York: Lucis Publishing Co., 1950.

Hodson, Geoffrey. *The Brotherhood of Angels and of Men.* London: Theosophical Publishing House, 1957.

Parisen, Maria, ed. *Angels and Mortals: Their Co-Creative Power.* Wheaton, Ill.: Quest Books, 1990.

Rosa, José Alberto, with Nathaniel Altman. *Finding Your Personal Power Spots.* London: Aquarian Press, 1983.

Schimmel, Annemarie. *Mystical Dimensions of Islam.* Chapel Hill: University of North Carolina Press, 1975.

Southern Centre of Theosophy. *Devas and Men.* Adyar, India: The Theosophical Publishing House, 1977.


## Chapter 9

Decter, Jacqueline. *Nicholas Roerich.* Rochester, Vt.: Park Street Press, 1989.

The Findhorn Community. *The Findhorn Garden.* New York: HarperCollins, 1975.

Kaplan, Rachel, and Steven Kaplan. *The Experience of Nature.* New York: Cambridge University Press, 1989.

Kunz, Dora Van Gelder. *Angels and Devas.* Audiotape. Craryville, N.Y.: Pumpkin Hollow Farm, n.d.

Southern Centre of Theosophy. *Devas and Men.* Adyar, India: The Theosophical Publishing House, 1977.

Tompkins, Peter, and Christopher Bird. *The Secret Life of Plants.* New York: Harper & Row, 1973.

Wright, Machaelle Small. *Perelandra Garden Workbook.* Jeffersonton, Va.: Perelandra, Ltd., 1987.

Wright, Patricia C., and Richard D. Wright. *The Divining Heart.* Rochester, Vt.: Destiny Books, 1994.

## Chapter 10

Earthsave Foundation. *Our Food Our World.* Santa Cruz, Calif.: Earthsave Foundation, 1992.

Epstein, Donald, with Nathaniel Altman. *The Twelve Stages of Healing.* San Rafael: New World Library, 1994.

Hodson, Geoffrey. *The Brotherhood of Angels and of Men.* London: The Theosophical Publishing House, 1957.

# Resources

## Centers for Devic Research

The Findhorn Community
The Park
Forres IV36 0TZ
Scotland
A spiritual community in the north of Scotland, Findhorn offers classes, workshops, and publications on co-creating with nature and other New Age themes.

Perelandra, Ltd.
PO Box 3603
Warrenton, VA 22186
USA
A private community with a famous garden. While unannounced visits are not encouraged, Perelandra offers yearly seminars and a selection of literature, tapes, and flower essences prepared with devic collaboration.

## Visiting Native American Cultures

Journeys into American Indian Territory
PO Box 929
Westhampton Beach, NY 11978
USA
Offers study tours providing direct access to the life of NativeAmerican communities, including the Comanche, Kiowa, Arapaho, Apache, Ojibway,

and Puma. Tour members camp in tipis and other traditional native houses, learn tribal dances, eat traditional foods, participate in ceremonies, and learn traditional beliefs.

## Recommended Books and Tapes

Nathaniel Altman. *Sacred Trees* (Sierra Club Books, 1994). A book about humanity's special relationship with trees throughout history. The book was inspired and organized through contact with devas and nature spirits. Includes many old and rare illustrations of trees.

The Findhorn Community. *The Findhorn Garden* (New York: Harper-Collins, 1975). A classic book about the Findhorn Garden and the community's unique work with devic beings.

Marian Green. *The Elements of Natural Magic* (Rockport, Mass.: Element Books, 1989). A practical guide to help us attune to nature, celebrate the seasons, and use magic as a power for positive change.

Geoffrey Hodson. *The Brotherhood of Angels and of Men* (London: The Theosophical Publishing House, 1957). First published in 1927, this inspiring book contains some of the first messages received by Hodson from members of the angelic kingdom. Hodson's *The Kingdom of the Gods* (Adyar, India: The Theosophical Publishing House, 1970), is a classic book about the devic realms, written by the noted teacher and sensitive and richly illustrated with color drawings based on his clairvoyant observations. *Clairvoyant Investigations* (Wheaton, Ill.: Quest Books, 1987) can be considered a second volume to *The Kingdom of the Gods,* with observations from Hodson's later notebooks. It includes color illustrations of devas painted by various artists.

Dora Van Gelder Kunz. *Angels and Devas* and *Trees and Self-Confidence* (Pumpkin Hollow Farm, RR#1, Box 135, Craryville, NY 12521). Two audiotapes of informal presentations given at a theosophical camp by the renowned clairvoyant and codeveloper of the Therapeutic Touch healing modality.

Dorothy Maclean. *To Honor the Earth* (San Francisco: Harper-SanFrancisco, 1991). A beautiful book of inspiring messages from nature spirits as received by Maclean, accompanied by stunning photographs of plants, mountains, lakes, and landscapes by Kathleen Thormond Carr.

Maria Parisen, ed. *Angels and Mortals; Their Co-Creative Power* (Wheaton, Ill.: Quest Books, 1990). A comprehensive collection of essays on members of the angelic realms and our relationship to them.

Elizabeth Roberts and Elias Amidon, eds. *Earth Prayers* (New York: HarperCollins, 1991). An impressive compilation of Earth prayers from around the world.

José Alberto Rosa, with Nathaniel Altman. *Finding Your Personal Power Spots* (London: Aquarian Press, 1986). A guide to contacting our inner power spots as well as our outer power spots in nature. Based in part on the traditional Candomblé teachings of Brazil.

Molly Sheehan. *A Guide to Green Hope Farm: Flower Essences* (Meridan, N.H.: Green Hope Farm, 1994). This well-researched book is a guide to using flower essences, but it also contains information on how devas can assist healing.

Southern Centre of Theosophy. *Devas and Men* (Adyar, India; The Theosophical Publishing House, 1977). An extensive compilation of theosophical studies on the angelic kingdom by a group of Australian students. Includes some color illustrations.

Machaelle Small Wright. *Behaving As If the God in All Life Mattered* (Jeffersonton, Va.: Perelandra Ltd., 1987). This book on New Age ecology describes Wright's early experiences with devas and nature spirits and includes insights on the plant and animal kingdoms. Wright's *Perelandra Garden Workbook* (Jeffersonton, Va.: Perelandra, Ltd., 1987) is a complete guide to gardening with devas and nature spirits written by the founder of Perelandra, a unique center for nature research in the Findhorn tradition.

# Index